World Religions
DeMYSTiFieD®

Ebrahim E. I. Moosa, PhD
with Matt Cleary

McGraw
Hill
Education

New York   Chicago   San Francisco   Athens   London   Madrid   Mexico City
Milan   New Delhi   Singapore   Sydney   Toronto

1 2 3 4 5 6 7 8 9 10   QFR/QFR   1 0 9 8 7 6 5 4

ISBN   978-0-07-177022-4
MHID   0-07-177022-4

e-ISBN   978-0-07-177023-1
e-MHID   0-07-177023-2

Library of Congress Control Number: 2011936492

McGraw-Hill Education products are available at special quantity discounts to use as premiums and sales promotions or for use in corporate training programs. To contact a representative, please visit the Contact Us pages at www.mhprofessional.com.

Contents

Introduction

Demystifying Religion: Why Now? Why Here? Why Bother?

Some skeptics argue that any attempt to demystify world religions is unjustifiable, doomed to failure, or both. They ask questions like, Aren't matters of faith inherently subjective, and therefore mysterious to outsiders? Shouldn't we simply accept the reality that unfamiliar religious issues can be controversial (and perhaps even dangerous) to any who attempt to resolve their mysteries? Isn't religion itself inherently ambiguous . . . and best left that way?

This book assumes that the best answer to these questions is no. Like the other books in the Demystified series, it is designed as a classroom adjunct for students who are taking courses on the subject at the college level; given the topic we have chosen, however, we think what follows will also be useful for curious armchair learners of all ages and backgrounds. Regardless of whether you're studying for a course, this book begins from the premise that the more you learn about unfamiliar aspects of any faith tradition (whether it's yours or someone else's) the better off you are. There are two main reasons for this approach.

First, we live in a time when violence, conflict, and social instability—whether on the local, national, or international level—are increasingly perceived as connected to the way people worship (or don't). Whether that perception is accurate or inaccurate in our own personal experience is irrelevant; many people are now willing to do truly terrible things in the name of all the major religions. Even if we ourselves have not experienced this—even if we ourselves have no settled, formal approach to worship—even if we personally decline the possibility of worship altogether—the stakes are high, and ignorance makes them higher still.

Second, the question of what "religion" actually means is itself deeply unsettled, and that appears to be part of the problem. A common modern Western perception is that religion is a private matter, separate from larger society, and not something to be mixed with, say, politics or education. Many people in cultures outside of the United States, Europe, and Australia, however, are likely to view their own beliefs, rituals of worship, and spiritual practice as part of a common life and not a private belief. Indeed, many believers have been inclined to view the separation of "religious" values from "other" values as a profound cultural shock that has been accelerating in various ways for at least a century.

We believe these two issues are interrelated. We believe that the instability is intensified by the cultural divide over whether there is or should be a private realm for religion, and vice versa. We believe that a great gap has been widening. What's more, we believe that the only responsible—and perhaps the only sane—response to this dynamic is to demystify each major faith system in as many of its particulars as possible.

To demystify religion is simply to acknowledge and honor the possibility of differing perspectives. To demystify means to ask questions about perspective: Who is speaking? Who is naming things in and about a given religion? Often, we find that we face the age-old insider/outsider problem. A participant's viewpoint is called *emic*, to use the terminology of the social scientist. In contrast, the view of a nonparticipant or an outsider is called *etic*. To demystify is to illuminate as many of the potential blind spots arising from these differing perspectives as possible, to support efforts that enhance mutual understanding about faith and worship and advance the common good. This has more to do with tolerance and respect than it does with division and discord.

The timeline of our young twenty-first century already suggests that humanity has far more blind spots related to this subject than necessary. The more blind spots remain about how people around the world worship, and why they believe as they do, the deeper the mystery—and the greater the potential for paranoia, extremism, and mistrust.

Responsible demystification is the only way we know of to cast light on such blind spots. And that is what we aim to undertake here. Responsible demystification means learning about other faiths with empathy—identifying with and showing understanding for the feelings, motives, and situations of others—and not make hasty judgments about others without proper information, knowledge, and understanding. Demystification takes courage, but it is worth the effort because it means more information, more knowledge, and more understanding of the religions of the world.

How to Use This Book

Each chapter ends with a quiz that will help you to evaluate your understanding of the material covered. The quizzes are open-book quizzes—you should use the content of the chapter as a resource for determining the correct answers. A good suggestion is to achieve a score of at least 80 percent—eight out of ten correct answers—before going on to the next chapter. You will also find end-of-section tests that will help you to identify any problem areas before you move on to the next section of the book. If you score less than 80 percent on any portion of these end-of-section tests, you will want to go back and review the material on the religious tradition in question.

From time to time, you will encounter boxes entitled "Key Terms Demystified." These help you gain a deeper understanding of potentially unfamiliar terms and concepts. You'll also find sections called "Careful!" These highlight potential areas for misinterpretation in a given faith system. You'll also see boxes marked "Spiritually Speaking." These give you insights from trusted sources on particular issues relevant to the faith system under discussion.

The book ends with a Final Exam. This is your measuring tool to determine how well you have demystified the faith systems we've examined here. This exam contains 100 questions, and a good score on the Final Exam would be 75 percent or above.

A final piece of advice: Enjoy! That's the surest way to illuminate blind spots, and the best way to demystify anything.

Part One

The Indus and Beyond: Hinduism, Buddhism, Taoism, and Shinto

What was the first religion? No one knows. There is no one place you can visit and truthfully say, "Human religion starts here, now." There is, however, a place that connects to the earliest religious practices we know of, and that is the Indus River Valley.

The Indus River Valley Civilization extended across present-day Pakistan and northwest India. Archaeological evidence shows that this civilization dates back to roughly 3300 BCE. It comprised some of the biggest human habitations of the ancient world and served as an important crossroads of history, commerce, and empire. Here, we know, the complex faith system known as Hinduism emerged during what is now known as the Vedic period—but how and when remain puzzling questions without complete answers.

No belief system we know of precedes this civilization. A long series of reactions, counterreactions, and parallel religious movements followed, chronologically, the perpetually unfolding story of Hinduism that extends from this point. Among these later arrivals are the important faith systems of Buddhism, Taoism, and Shinto, each of which claim comparably long lineages, but none of which can claim to be older. That makes the Indus River a good place for us to begin our journey through the universe of human belief.

chapter **1**

Hinduism: History and Context

When you complete this chapter, you will be able to explain how the history of Hinduism differs from the history of other major faith systems.

CHAPTER OBJECTIVES

In this chapter, you will learn about:

- Where the word *Hinduism* comes from—and why it can be dangerous

- Religious creativity and pluralism on the Indian subcontinent

- Three historically unique features of Hinduism

- Five periods of development and evolution within the faith

We begin at the beginning, which means we begin with the world's longest-lived religious system still in operation: Hinduism.

Or perhaps it would be better to say we begin with "Hinduism," in quotation marks. Hinduism, after all, is simply the word we use now to describe a staggering variety of native religious practices that have arisen over the centuries in the Indian subcontinent.

For their own convenience, scholars gathered these practices together under one convenient umbrella term: *Hinduism*. The word derives from the Indus River, which supported the ancient Indus River Valley Civilization (3300 BCE to 1500 BCE), and which runs through the part of the world we would today call Pakistan. It is thought that the first part of the early Vedic period, from which the earliest Hindu scriptures date, coincides with the final centuries of the Indus River Valley Civilization.

Naming a religion after this historically important river makes sense up to a point, but it is also a little like gathering together every form of worship that has ever been practiced within a hundred miles of the Thames River in England and calling that conglomeration "Thamesism."

KEY TERMS DEMYSTIFIED: Indus River Valley Civilization (3300 BCE to 1500 BCE)

A civilization comprising some of the biggest human habitations of the ancient world. It was located in sections of present-day Pakistan and India.

Instead of using the word *Hinduism*, we might be more accurate if we described what we are talking about in this section of the book as "the long legacy, and new expression, of religious tradition originating in and around India, from at least the Iron Age forward." A phrase like that is too cumbersome for people to remember or use, though. So we are probably stuck with the current globally accepted label. But we should remember that Hinduism differs profoundly from other major religious traditions not only in its age but also in its diversity.

KEY TERMS DEMYSTIFIED: Hinduism

The long legacy, and new expression, of religious tradition originating in and around India, from at least the Iron Age forward.

Careful! *The label of* Hinduism *was, we must always remember, coined by outsiders. That name was only born in the nineteenth century. Each and every time we use the phrase, we should remind ourselves that it is, like other umbrella terms—such as* literature *or* Europeans *or* popular culture*—potentially dangerous because it covers so much ground. While the term* Hinduism *is useful in certain settings, it is also likely to make us forget, now and then, the hazards of using it to make broad generalizations. It is far too easy to overlook the extraordinary diversity it reflects.*

The practices within this faith system are so diverse, and cover such a vast historical canvas, that even the seemingly simple task of understanding Hinduism's core principles and beliefs (the subject of our next chapter) can be a challenging one. To understand why this is so, we need a little historical background. Providing that background, as painlessly as possible, is the goal here.

SPIRITUALLY SPEAKING

"India is the meeting place of the religions and among these Hinduism alone is by itself a vast and complex thing, not so much a religion as a great diversified and yet subtly unified mass of spiritual thought, realization and aspiration."

—*Sri Aurobindo, Indian nationalist and spiritual reformer*

The Paradox

Let's start with a paradox. This, the dictionary tells us, is "a statement that appears to contradict itself." The paradox about this faith system is: Hinduism is so old that it is new.

This simultaneously old-and-new reality seems to me to be unique to Hinduism. It is as good a point of entry as any to our discussion of this massively influential collection of traditions. How can Hinduism be so old that it is new? The answer is that it is simultaneously the world's most ancient surviving set of religious beliefs and a vigorous, flexible, contemporary modern religious experience. Threads of its observance extend through its history more or less unchanged for thousands of years. It has survived as long as it has because of its ability to adapt, to consolidate, to tolerate multiple strains, to live and let live.

Hinduism's ability to adapt, to accept multiple cultures and viewpoints, reflects a profoundly modern attitude, one that is not as obviously woven into the historical fabric of other major faith systems. And this adaptability is one of the keys to the faith's astonishingly long history.

SPIRITUALLY SPEAKING

"Hinduism has proven much more open than any other religion to new ideas, scientific thought, and social experimentation. Many concepts like reincarnation, meditation, yoga and others have found worldwide acceptance. It would not be surprising to find Hinduism the dominant religion of the twenty-first century. It would be a religion that doctrinally is less clear-cut than mainstream Christianity, politically less determined than Islam, ethically less heroic than Buddhism, but it would offer something to everybody. It will appear idealistic to those who look for idealism, pragmatic to the pragmatists, spiritual to the seekers, sensual to the here-and-now generation. Hinduism, by virtue of its lack of an ideology and its reliance on intuition, will appear to be more plausible than those religions whose doctrinal positions petrified a thousand years ago."

—*Klaus L. Klostermeier, researcher on Hinduism and Indian history and culture*

The ancient adaptive roots of this faith system are what make the contemporary, modern reality of Hinduism possible. Perhaps, when we say "Hinduism," what we really mean is the instinct of native religious creativity and pluralism in and around India.

So: If one's way of experiencing connection with the Divine has originated in the Indian subcontinent, and if one is willing to coexist with, or perhaps even connect one's practices to, others in the region who are inclined to worship differently, then one's system of beliefs may well become less dogmatic, richer, and more relevant—all as a result of one's willingness to accept multiple viewpoints, to accept diversity in belief and practice.

When it is understood in this way, Hinduism becomes a complex *network* of native beliefs, a network that charts interesting connections, does not attempt to resolve every difference, encourages new ideas and expressions within the native Indian tradition, and permits countless paths to the Divine. At the same time, the network requires acceptance of a comparatively few core concepts—the doctrine of reincarnation, for instance—of those wishing to join the network. This historical willingness to embrace and encompass multiple theological viewpoints on major questions of doctrine is unique to Hinduism.

KEY TERMS DEMYSTIFIED: **Reincarnation**

The rebirth of the soul in a new body after death.

Brief Timeline of Hinduism

Circa 2800 BCE	The Indus Valley civilization thrives.
1200–900 BCE	The early Vedic period, in which the oldest Vedas are compiled. (The Vedas are the primary texts of Hinduism.)
900–600 BCE	The late Vedic period. Brahmanic worship emerges, and with it a focus on ritualism and social duties.
800–300 BCE	During this period the major Upanishads are composed, emphasizing principles of karma and reincarnation.
Circa 550 BCE	Jainism is founded.
Circa 520 BCE	Buddhism is founded.
500 BCE	A vast but distinct period of roughly a millennium and a half begins at this point, during which devotional movements focused on Shiva, Vishnu,

	and Devi take form, and epics and Puranas (eulogies devoted to a specific deity) are composed.
Circa 320–185 BCE	The Mauryan dynasty—India's first empire— establishes control of almost the entire Indian subcontinent. An important ruler during this period was Ashoka the Great (269–232 BCE).
Circa 320–500 CE	Rise of the Gupta Empire.
Circa 500–650 CE	The Gupta Empire divides into several kingdoms.
Circa 600–1600 CE	During this period a number of important devotional movements arise, including those based on the Tantras, a set of esoteric meditation and worship rituals aiming to expand energy and transform consciousness.
1526 CE	The Mughal Empire, most of whose leaders were Muslim, is established.
17th–19th centuries CE	The Hindu Renaissance.
1720	The Mughal Empire begins a prolonged collapse; the British begin to take power.
1857	The National War of Independence against the British begins; it fails to secure its stated goal.
1876	Queen Victoria is named Empress of India.
1895	Vivekananda forms the Vedanta Society, advocating for Hinduism as a world religion and India as an independent nation.
1915	Mahatma Gandhi begins work on behalf of the Indian nationalist movement.
1947	Led by figures such as Mahatma Gandhi, India regains independence from the British; however, its partitioning leads to violence among Hindus, Muslims, and Sikhs.
1948	Mahatma Gandhi is assassinated.
1950	The Constitution of the Republic of India takes effect.

Three Historical Singularities

Three important historical quirks, found only in this faith system, are essential to any meaningful understanding of it.

This first of these is that Hinduism has no single founder. Unlike other major religions whose origin can be traced to a single compelling leader, Hinduism has no such figure at its center.

The second unique historical reality about Hinduism, and the one that is most likely to befuddle historians of religion, is that Hinduism has no known starting point. We cannot say when it began; we can only say when its earliest traces may (or may not) have been discovered by archaeologists, which appears to be something like four and a half millennia ago. Even these artifacts, however, are subjects of intense scholarly debate.

And the third unique historical reality has to do with the long history of the Indian subcontinent. There is a long history of tension and dynamic growth from the interaction of existing and established cultures in this part of the world. Time and again, we see this faith system evolving in response to its new contacts with emerging cultures, ideas, and institutions. I will explore these influences in more depth in the next chapter, but the following table summarizes the five main periods of history that reflect this pattern.

KEY TERMS DEMYSTIFIED: Yoga and Karma

Yoga is an umbrella term describing a wide variety of mental, physical, and spiritual disciplines, all deriving from ancient India and all meant to deliver a state of permanent peace.

Karma is action regarded as triggering inevitable good or bad results for the person who performs it, either in this life or in a later incarnation.

Hinduism's Response to Emerging Cultures, Ideas, and Institutions

Five Periods of Interaction with Other Cultures	Hinduism's Response
Vedic Period (1500 BCE–500 BCE)	
Emergence of Aryan culture in the Indus River Valley, either by migration or a process of slow cultural transformation.	Compilation of earliest scriptures, the Vedas. Emergence of priestly class.
Classical or Golden Age (500 BCE–500 CE)	
Emergence of Buddhism and Jainism on the Indian subcontinent.	Compilation of a new wave of scriptures incorporating important literary and devotional responses to these new faiths; minimization of fire sacrifice ritual; emphasis on temple worship. Emphasis and development of the idea of karma. Consolidation of the discipline of yoga.
Medieval Period (500 CE–1500 CE)	
Collapse of Gupta Empire; rise of regional kingdoms with diverse religious traditions. Rise of Islam as both a religious and political force.	Emergence of a network of great regional temples; rise of the practice of devotion (*bhakti*) to major deities within these temples. Establishment of Sanskrit as a culturally uniting written language. Principle of equality of devotees begins to win adherents.
Pre-Modern Period (1500 CE–1750 CE)	
Europeans explore, share their culture with, and begin the quest to dominate the Indian subcontinent.	The city of Pune is established as a seat of religious learning and practice. New devotional emphasis on worship of "a god without qualities" appears in northern India.
British Period (c. 1750 CE–1947 CE)	
The Mughal Empire falls (1757); British rule follows.	The so-called Hindu Renaissance begins. Reformers, tapping into growing public resentment over British dominance, advocate a return to "eternal law," the eradication of perceived superstitions, and an emphasis on ethical principles, Indian nationalism, and missionary work.

Summary

- The label *Hinduism* was coined by outsiders in the nineteenth century.

- This label describes a staggering variety of native religious practices that have arisen over the centuries in the Indian subcontinent.

- Hinduism is so old that it is new. Hinduism's ability to adapt and to accept multiple cultures and viewpoints reflects a profoundly modern attitude that differs from the historical fabric of other major faith systems. This adaptability is one of the keys to the faith's astonishingly long history.

- "Hinduism" encompasses the instinct of native religious creativity and pluralism in and around India.

- Hinduism has no single founder and no known starting point.

- This faith system has continually evolved in response to its new contacts with emerging cultures, ideas, and institutions.

QUIZ

1. **Hinduism has**
   A. a single founder dating from the Mughal period.
   B. no one historical founder because it dates back to ancient interactions of cultures and traditions on the Indian subcontinent.
   C. a creative belief system under which a single founder of the religion lives forever but perpetually seeks anonymity in the guise of a non-Hindu.
   D. None of the above.

2. **Karma is**
   A. the impossibility of being reborn.
   B. action regarded as triggering inevitable good or bad results for the person who performs it, either in this life or in a later incarnation.
   C. the belief that there is one God.
   D. None of the above.

3. **Yoga is**
   A. a North American missionary movement designed to convert people to Hinduism.
   B. a creative combination of Hinduism and Christianity.
   C. a discipline that combines religion and contemporary cuisine.
   D. None of the above.

4. **Which was NOT a factor in the history of Hinduism?**
   A. Responses to the Aryan culture
   B. Responses to the Rastafari movement
   C. Responses to British dominance
   D. None of the above

5. **The Hindu Renaissance was a response to**
   A. Aryan dominance.
   B. Mughal dominance.
   C. British dominance.
   D. None of the above.

6. **Hinduism is strongly associated with**

    A. the long history of the Indian subcontinent.

    B. the long history of North American native peoples.

    C. the long history of Australian nonscriptural nature worship.

    D. None of the above.

7. **The emergence of a priestly class can be traced to**

    A. the Vedic period.

    B. the Golden Age.

    C. the nineteenth century of the Common Era.

    D. None of the above.

8. **During the medieval period**

    A. the Iron Age emerged.

    B. the Gupta Empire collapsed.

    C. the Himalayas were colonized by Europeans.

    D. None of the above.

9. **Jainism refers to**

    A. modern Hindu handcrafts.

    B. worship of specific Hindu deities.

    C. a rigorous cycle of fasting.

    D. None of the above.

10. **The liturgical language of ancient Hinduism was**

    A. Greek.

    B. Urdu.

    C. Hindi.

    D. None of the above.

Hinduism: Core Beliefs and Practices

When you complete this chapter, you will be able to describe some of the most important beliefs and practices within Hinduism. You will also get a sense of the geographic placement of Hinduism's followers, the religion's size in comparison with other traditions, and the main forms of worship observed by Hindus.

CHAPTER OBJECTIVES

In this chapter, you will learn about:

- The size of the global Hindu population
- Three major Hindu sects
- The major Hindu scriptures
- Core Hindu beliefs
- Core Hindu worship practices

As vast, sprawling, and complex as it is, there are some core concepts and practices that are embraced virtually unanimously among Hindu practitioners, such as belief in reincarnation and belief in the principle of karma. This chapter will examine those beliefs and practices and give you a look at the best answers to the most common questions outsiders have about this religion.

CAREFUL! *What appears in this chapter is a summary of some, but not all, Hindu beliefs and practices. No brief summary of the "belief system" of this tradition is possible.*

Despite the word's having been coined relatively recently by non-Indians, this book will use *Hindu* from now on without prejudice. It is offered in its contemporary sense, which is now embraced by countless worshippers in India and elsewhere as being synonymous with the ancient Sanskrit phrase *Sanātana Dharma*. That translates, more or less, as "eternal law" or "eternal religion." Check out the definition box for more on the important concept of *dharma*.

KEY TERMS DEMYSTIFIED: Dharma

An extremely important term within Hinduism that covers a wide range of meanings. In most modern contexts, it can refer either to one's personal spiritual obligations based on factors such as age, social class, or gender; to one's capacity for upright behavior; or simply to one's religion. The word also carries an ancient meaning of "that which upholds or supports."

One translation of the critical phrase *Sanātana Dharma* might be "the eternal law that preserves."

Like Hinduism itself, dharma is seen as having no beginning and no end.

The goal in posing and answering the following common questions about Hinduism is twofold: (1) to demystify some of the most common issues and questions people have about the faith system, and (2) to get you up and running with the faith's key concepts. Ready?

How Many Hindus Are There?

As with all the major global faiths, a single precise number is hard to come by, and the estimates that stand in its place are controversial. The best guesses range between 800 million and one billion people. That's a margin of error of 200 million people, which certainly sounds like a huge number, but bear in mind that this figure should be compared to a total world population of approximately seven billion as of this writing. If you count secularism (including atheism and agnosticism) as a category of religious identification, which many people do, the figure between the two estimates, 900 million, would make Hindus the world's fourth largest religious group, behind those affiliating with Christianity, Islam, and secularism.

Something like 80.5 percent of the entire world Hindu population lives in India, according to the CIA's World Factbook; large Hindu populations are also found in places like Nepal, Sri Lanka, Indonesia, Bangladesh, Malaysia, Mauritius, Pakistan, the Philippines, the United Kingdom, and the United States. Roughly 82 percent of all Indian nationals are Hindu.

What Are the Major Sects Within Hinduism?

Talking about "major sects" within Hinduism is a little like talking about the "major English-speaking countries." If you want to, you can identify England, the United States, and Canada to create a helpful, instantly accessible list of three "major" countries where that language is spoken predominantly, and such a list might be a useful beginning point for someone with no prior knowledge of the subject. At the same time, however, you would probably want to bear in mind that you were leaving out countries like Australia, Hong Kong, South Africa, the Philippines, and dozens of others.

There are so many religious subgroups within Hinduism that describing all of them responsibly is close to impossible in an overview book like this one. A few of the most notable and historically influential religious schools within Hinduism are discussed in this chapter, but please note that they are certainly not the *only* important schools of thought and practice! Consider them a starting point for your own future research.

With that disclaimer in place, we can begin.

Shaivism

Shaivism, also known as *Saivism* or *Shavism*, reveres the god Shiva as "creator, preserver, destroyer, revealer, and concealer of all that is," according to its adherents. The image of Shiva dancing in the form of many-armed Nataraja, standing on one leg, is a familiar, even iconic one. It's an image that most Westerners instantly associate with Hinduism, and perhaps even consider synonymous with it. The Katha Upanishad says of Shiva, "In His robe are woven heaven and earth, mind and body. . . . He is the bridge from death to deathless life."

The god Shiva, "creator, preserver, destroyer, revealer, and concealer of all that is".
Credit: McGraw-Hill Education

SPIRITUALLY SPEAKING

"Shaivism or Saivism is the name given to a group of religious traditions which regard Lord Siva, also spelled as Shiva, as the highest Supreme Self or Brahman. . . . [Shaivism] is considered to be one of the oldest, if not the oldest, sect of Hinduism. . . . Followers of Saivism are popularly known as Saivas or Saivites. The early Vedic Indians worshipped an aspect of Lord Siva, known as Rudra, whom they both feared and revered. In the later Vedic period some Upanishads emerged, such as the Sgvetasvatara Upanishad and the Katha Upanishad, in which Lord Siva was depicted as the highest Supreme Brahman."

—*Jayaram V. of Saivism.net*

KEY TERMS DEMYSTIFIED: Vedas, Sutras, Upanishads, and *Bhagavad Gita*

Vedas are both the oldest surviving examples of Indian literature and the oldest scriptures of Hinduism. They can be broken down into four separate texts, three of which (the Rigveda, the Yajurveda, and the Samaveda) relate to early Vedic sacrificial rites, and one of which (the Atharaveda) features hymns, spells, incantations, and other material.

The **Sutras** are brief sayings meant to preserve a given piece of instruction relating to the Vedas, or to convey some other important teaching. The **Upanishads** are a diverse collection of philosophical observations, initially conveyed in an oral tradition and compiled at various points in history. The *Bhagavad Gita* is an excerpt from the epic text known as the *Mahabharata*, regarded as one of the masterpieces of world literature. The text of the *Bhagavad Gita* presents the Lord Krishna as a divine teacher, in discussion with the prince Arjuna.

KEY TERMS DEMYSTIFIED: Brahma, Brahman, Brahmin

Brahma is the Hindu god of creation. The **Brahman** is the Hindu concept of the supreme spirit that transcends, is the origin of, and is the means of support for the universe. A **Brahmin** is a member of the highest caste, or social class, within Indian society.

Vaishnavism

Vaishnavism, also known as *Vaisnavism*, reveres the god Vishnu (and his many manifestations) as the original and all-powerful God. This reverence takes place from different points of view and through different traditions, appealing to God by such names as Narayana, Krishna, Vāsudeva, and, of course, Vishnu. Vaishnavism's distinctive devotional practices, notably Bhakti and Bhakti Yoga, are derived from a variety of sacred texts: the Upanishads, the *Bhagavad Gita*, and the Padma, Vishnu, and Bhagavata Puranas. In the *Bhagavad Gita*, having taken the form of Krishna, the god Vishnu says, "I am the goal, the sustainer, the master, the witness, the abode, the refuge, and the most dear friend. I am the creation and the annihilation, the basis of everything, the resting place and the eternal seed."

KEY TERMS DEMYSTIFIED: **Bhakti**

Bhakti is the active, loving, devotional activity of a worshipper toward the divine. Bhakti Yoga is a spiritual, mental, and physical discipline incorporating a personal attitude of love and devotion toward the Divine.

SPIRITUALLY SPEAKING

"The largest community within the family of religions called Hinduism worships God under the name of Vishnu ('one who is all-pervading'). Vaishnavas are divided into many smaller divisions, often focusing on one form or avatar (descent) of Vishnu. . . . The two focuses of veneration are Krishna and Rama, who are usually considered God, with other deities in relatively subordinate positions. Vaishnavas tend to be personalists, associated with the devotional, bhakti traditions. . . . From the twelfth century onwards a bhakti renaissance swept across India, bringing waves of devotional sentiment. Centers of devotion were rediscovered and revived in places such as Ayodhya and Vrindavana."

—*International Society for Krishna Consciousness (ISKCON, also known as the Hare Krishna movement)*

Shaktism

Shaktism is the third great devotional school within Hinduism. Its object of veneration is the ancient goddess figure Shakti, also known as Devi or Parvati, the Divine Mother celebrated as the "one without a second." Shakti is seen not only as the source of the created physical universe, but also as its dynamic embodiment and as the energy that guides it. She also transcends and embodies all pairs and opposites. As *Devi-Bhagavata Purana*, a central Shakta scripture, puts it:

"I am Manifest Divinity, Unmanifest Divinity, and Transcendent Divinity. I am Brahma, Vishnu, and Shiva, as well as Saraswati, Lakshmi, and Parvati. I am the Sun and I am the Stars, and I am also the Moon. I am all animals and birds, and I am the outcaste as well, and the thief. I am the low person of dreadful deeds, and the great person of excellent deeds. I am Female, I am Male, and I am Neuter."

SPIRITUALLY SPEAKING

"Since Shiva embodies the male principle and Shakti embodies the female, the two principles of Shaivism and Shaktism are complementary. Shakti doctrine tends to emphasise the non-difference between matter and spirit, and looks to the creative impetus of matter rather than its ability to delude and entangle. For this reason, Shaktas worship for material benefit as well as final liberation."

—*International Society for Krishna Consciousness (ISKCON, also known as the Hare Krishna movement)*

What Do Hindus Believe?

Given the remarkable and enduring diversity of the faith, it is probably safest to talk about what *most* Hindus believe. Those core beliefs can be summarized as follows.

- The Vedas are a divinely revealed source of guidance. These ancient hymns, humanity's oldest religious scriptures, are considered to have been revealed by the Almighty, and they serve as the foundation of all belief and practice.

- The universe goes through cycles of creation, sustenance, and annihilation. This process is repeated without end.

- Karma, the enduring law of cause and effect, guides personal destiny. If one dies while one's karma is unresolved, one is reborn into a new body. If one resolves one's karma, one can escape the cycle of rebirth and attains liberation (moksha).

- Guidance from a spiritually awakened teacher, or satguru, is an essential step on the journey toward one's own awakening. *Satguru* means "true guru." The term describes a saint or enlightened person.

- Meditation, self-assessment, pilgrimage, sound moral behavior, purification, and individual discipline are nonnegotiable requirements for those who wish to escape the cycle of birth and death, transcend their own experience, and encounter the divine.

- Divine beings are alive in worlds humans cannot see.

- Worship through rituals of personal and community devotion, whether carried out in one's household or in a temple, establishes a communion with these divine beings.

- Life is sacred and deserving of both respect and reverence. This guiding principle of respect for life is known as *ahimsa*.

- There are many authentic religious paths; all can be equally valid approaches to salvation.

- There are many manifestations of the divine, but one Supreme Being of transcendence (meaning "beyond categorization and description"), omnipresence (meaning "present everywhere"), and immanence (meaning "dwelling within each believer").

This last point brings us to an issue of considerable controversy: Is Hinduism monotheistic—that is, focused on worshipping a single God—or not? The best answer to this question (from the Hindu point of view) is probably something along the lines of "If you want."

It is primarily outsiders who have major difficulties with Hinduism's lack of a definitive answer to this question. As one astute student of religion once put the matter in an online essay, "the Indian mind is much more inclined [than the Western mind] to regard divergent views as complementary, rather than competing."

The -*theism* Issue

Is Hinduism polytheistic, monotheistic, or pantheistic? The effort to attach one and only one of these labels to the massive network of religious practices that is Hinduism has been going on for centuries. One can argue all three positions persuasively, and with ample evidence.

KEY TERMS DEMYSTIFIED: Polytheism, Monotheism, Pantheism

Polytheism is the worship of many gods. **Monotheism** is the worship of one God. **Pantheism** is the worship of the Universe (or Nature) in all its manifestations, or the belief that everything is divine.

A polytheistic (worship of many gods) tradition within Hinduism is easy to spot, given the huge pantheon of deities it accepts. Hindu devotees may worship different deities based on the situation, needs, and requirements of their lives at a given moment, and are likely to praise and glorify the deities worshipped by other believers.

Much contemporary Hindu practice, however, emphasizes a monotheistic viewpoint that sees all these various gods as diverse manifestations of the one Supreme God. "Hindus believe in monotheistic polytheism, rather than polytheism," explains a post on the website The Hindu Universe.

To complete the confusion, there is an emphasis throughout many of Hinduism's religious and philosophical texts insisting that the Divine is literally to be found everywhere, and that the Creator and the Creation are in fact identical. This is a classic tenet of pantheistic thought, one that is explicitly rejected by some other faiths (Islam, for instance).

In the end, the best answer to the question, "Is Hinduism polytheistic, monotheistic, or pantheistic?" may well be "Take your pick."

How Do Hindus Worship?

There are five important worship obligations accepted by virtually all Hindus. They are:

- *Dharma* (meaning "virtuous life, life within divinely established guidelines") is morally correct, selfless conduct that respects all living beings.

- *Upsana* (usually translated as "devotion" or "worship") is everyday practice, whether it takes place in the home at a special shrine room, in the temple, or elsewhere. This practice might take the form of chanting, study, yogic practices, or simply sitting quietly in front of a small devotional table in quest of serenity.

- *Utsava* (meaning "holy days") is worship through participation in festivals and through temple attendance on Mondays, Fridays, and recognized days of special observance.

- *Tirthayatra* (meaning "pilgrimage") is the act of taking a spiritually inspired journey from one place to another.

- *Samskara* (typically translated as "rites of passage") is the ceremonial observance of important life events such as birth, marriage, and death.

What Is the Original Language of Hinduism?

Classical Sanskrit, following grammatical rules traceable to the fourth century BCE, is this faith system's liturgical language. Sanskrit is to modern Hindi as precursor languages like Latin and Greek are to modern European languages. Sanskrit's use in a primarily devotional context—in hymns and mantras, for instance—is comparable to the important role Latin still plays in certain Roman Catholic rites. Unlike Latin, however, there are occasional attempts to revive Sanskrit as a popular modern language. It is classified as one of the official languages of the northern Indian state of Uttarakhand (along with Hindi) and is spoken in modern dialect in a handful of villages as a primary language. Sanskrit's survival in any form is a remarkable testament to its enduring influence on culture and society in the region, considering the ancient language's status as one of the earliest confirmed members of the Indo-European language family.

KEY TERMS DEMYSTIFIED: Sanskrit and Mantra

Sanskrit is the ancient language of Hinduism. A **mantra** is a sound or group of words repeated with the aim of creating or supporting a spiritual transformation.

The OM symbol represents a *mantra*, a prayerful transformational phrase, sacred within the Hindu tradition, Buddhism, and Jainism.

Credit: Image Source/Getty Images

Sanskrit is also a liturgical language in the faiths of Buddhism and Jainism, both of which arose in reaction to movements within Hinduism. Each of these two religious schools has a complex and unique relationship with the Hindu religious tradition.

Who Leads the Hindus?

The definitively decentralized faith, Hinduism has no formal hierarchical leadership system, and in this, it contrasts sharply with "top-down" branches of Christianity such as Roman Catholicism and with the hierarchically structured schools of practice to be found within the Shia sect of Islam.

Recall that Hinduism has no historical founder. Its followers are likely to respond to questions about who "leads" or "directs" the faith with an explanation that the Sanātana Dharma needs no human leadership, given its status as the Eternal Religion that neither begins nor ends. If anything "leads" Hinduism, followers might argue, it would be the most ancient scriptures, the Vedas—or perhaps Brahman, the ultimate reality.

Although there is no human leader of all the Hindus, we should acknowledge the traditional role of the *guru*, the wise person with experience and authority in a certain area of human affairs to guide others. The concept is an extremely flexible one within Hindu practice and may be applied to any individual who attracts and guides followers and assumes the role of a teacher—or even to inanimate objects such as books. The term *satguru*, however, applies specifically to an enlightened spiritual teacher.

KEY TERMS DEMYSTIFIED: Guru

A wise person with experience and authority in a certain area of human affairs.

Hinduism in a Box	
Divinity	There is one Supreme Reality (Brahman). Brahman is manifested in many entities.
Afterlife	Reincarnation follows death. The cycle of birth and death must continue as long as karma is unresolved. This cycle continues until one attains liberation and is united with the Supreme Reality.
Purpose of Human Life	Human beings are prisoners of their own delusion and ignorance. Disciplined spiritual practice can eventually bring about a release from this imprisonment, or, in the meantime, reincarnation in a better state.
Distinctive Practices and Beliefs	Yoga Meditation Vegetarianism (emphasized by major schools, but not universally observed) Cow considered holy, strongly associated with Krishna
Outsiders Often Distracted by	Caste system (religiously sanctioned system of social classes identifying four groups—priests, nobles/warriors, artisans/craftsmen, laborers—and one outsider group of "untouchables") Monotheism/polytheism debate

Summary

- Hinduism's size and astonishing diversity do not prevent it from embracing core beliefs that virtually all of its adherents accept. Among these are belief in reincarnation, belief in the principle of karma, and the status of the Vedas as divinely revealed scriptures.

- Hinduism can be seen as polytheistic, monotheistic, or pantheistic, depending on your own situation and perspective.

QUIZ

1. **Important Hindu scriptures include**
   A. the Vedas.
   B. Brahma.
   C. the Gospels.
   D. None of the above.

2. **Three important Hindu deities are**
   A. Brahma, Brahman, and Brahmin.
   B. Indus, Indi, and Inda.
   C. Siva, Vishnu, and Shakti.
   D. None of the above.

3. **The ancient language of Hinduism is**
   A. classical Sanskrit.
   B. Arabic.
   C. Hindi.
   D. None of the above.

4. **Bhakti is**
   A. the active, loving devotional activity of a worshipper toward the Divine.
   B. a Mughal tradition having nothing to do with Hinduism.
   C. a kind of devotional dance performed only by contemporary English Hindus.
   D. None of the above.

5. **A mantra is**
   A. a kind of garment.
   B. a military saint.
   C. a sound or group of words repeated with the aim of creating or supporting a spiritual transformation.
   D. None of the above.

6. **Upsana is**
   A. everyday practice, whether it takes place in the home at a special shrine room, in the temple, or elsewhere.
   B. a text of Buddhism.
   C. a religious epic dating from the fourth century of the Common Era.
   D. None of the above.

7. **Tirthayatra is**

    A. a set of special prayer beads.
    B. the act of taking a spiritually inspired journey from one place to another.
    C. a Nepalese saint.
    D. None of the above.

8. **Samskara is**

    A. the ceremonial observance of important life events such as birth, marriage, and death.
    B. a levitating temple located near the Ganges River.
    C. the name of a leading politician of the Gupta Empire.
    D. None of the above.

9. **Hindus believe that**

    A. reincarnation is a fact of existence.
    B. reincarnation is impossible.
    C. reincarnation is limited to human beings.
    D. None of the above.

10. **Brahman is held by Hindus to be**

    A. a deity within the Hindu Trinity.
    B. manifested in many entities.
    C. a social class.
    D. None of the above.

chapter 3

Buddhism: History and Context

When you complete this chapter, you will be able to explain the main events in the history of Buddhism, including the life of the Buddha and the emergence of the main schools.

CHAPTER OBJECTIVES

In this chapter, you will learn about:

- The story of Buddhism
- The Buddha
- What an ethical religion is
- What Theravada Buddhism is
- What Mahayana Buddhism is
- What Vajrayana Buddhism is

Buddhism's story has two points of entry. The first is the life story of its founder Gautama Buddha, which is one of the great religious narratives in human history; the second is the more complex story of the enduring, multifaceted religious tradition that claims him as its central figure. Both of those stories are important if you aim to demystify this belief system.

Japanese statue of the Buddha.

Credit: Tom Bonaventure/Getty Images

Understanding and balancing both of these stories is the business of this chapter. Implementing them into one's life is the work of the believer, and perhaps the work of a lifetime. In this chapter, you'll get a responsible overview of each story, and some thoughts on how they relate to each other.

The Prince

The story of the Buddha comes from a period so long ago—five centuries before Jesus, or maybe a little less—that modern standards about what is and isn't "historically accurate" are not particularly helpful or relevant. Our access to history is not helpful here in the way that it becomes helpful in discussions of later figures like Jesus and Muhammad. With those figures, we can ask, "What really happened to this person during his life?" and we are likely to get some clear, or at least plausible, answers.

> ## KEY TERMS DEMYSTIFIED: **Buddha**
>
> "Awakened One" or "Enlightened One."

Buddhism is different from Islam and Christianity in this regard. When we ask what really happened to the Buddha, the historical answers are a good deal less confident. Yet that is not as large a problem as it might appear. Buddhism is an ethical religion that de-emphasizes belief in a deity such as Yahweh or Allah, or revelations proceeding from such a deity. Instead, an ethical religion promotes ethical and moral principles that can assist a believer in the goal of attaining greater harmony with the universe. Because it claims no moment of divine historical intervention in human affairs, the historical markers for Buddhism are perhaps not as relevant as for some of the other faiths we will be examining.

An ethical religion is one that emphasizes the pursuit of virtuous or exemplary behavior over a belief in a deity. Buddhism, Taoism, and Confucianism have been classified as ethical religions.

What We Know

We can say with some certainty that a man who came to be known during his own lifetime as the Buddha was born, reached maturity, renounced the world, became a spiritual seeker, experienced an awakening, became a revered teacher, attracted followers, and died. And we know that this all played out in an area we would today call Nepal, near the northern Indian border.

Beyond that, we are in debt to accounts of his life and teachings that have been passed down by the Buddha's followers, accounts that were not formalized in written form for centuries.

We are left, then, with a story about a remarkable man that occasionally uses material that can't be verified. The story is probably more important for what it teaches us about the guiding principles of Buddhism than anything else, because some of the details of the Buddha's life will probably never be known for sure. But since the man in question, the Buddha, is widely regarded as one of the most influential figures in human history—the historian Michael Hart ranked him at number four, above figures like Confucius and St. Paul—the story that has come down to us is important and worth understanding. I will share its most widely accepted version.

Early Life

Long before he was known as the Buddha, the man we are interested in was known as Siddhārtha Gautama. He was born into a royal family; his father, the king, was the ruler of an important feudal realm, and the land he led was prosperous. Siddhārtha's mother died shortly after the boy was born, and he was raised by his aunt, the second wife of the king.

A holy man declared that the king's son would grow up to be either a great religious sage or a great ruler. The king, who wished for his son to succeed him as the ruler of the nation, resolved to do everything he possibly could to make the royal life appealing to his son, and so did his best to ensure that Siddhārtha be provided with a life that included every imaginable luxury—and excluded every form of human suffering. The little boy grew up having no knowledge of poverty, sickness, old age, or death. Whenever he left the palace, these realities were shielded from him, on the king's orders.

Despite having married a beautiful woman, Yasodhara, who bore him a son, Siddhārtha grew restless and unhappy in the palace, and eventually made his way out of it unprotected. Beyond the palace walls, he encountered three realities that shocked him profoundly: an old man bent over and trembling (Siddhārtha had never seen an old man before), a man who was seriously ill (Siddhārtha had never seen physical illness, either), and a corpse being carried to the funeral pyre (he had had no idea that people died). Later, he saw a monk who wandered the land and lived the life of strict austerity and deprivation held in high esteem by many of the most advanced practitioners of the Hindu faith. In the monk's eyes, the prince saw a peace and acceptance that led him to believe that perhaps he could single-mindedly solve the riddle of human suffering—by following the glow in the old monk's eyes. Presumably that meant following the path of the ascetic.

KEY TERMS DEMYSTIFIED: **Ascetic**

Someone who abstains from all indulgence.

Not long after that, the prince renounced his royal life, left his father, his wife, and his child behind, and exited the palace. His goal: to learn the origin of human suffering—and how it may be overcome by anyone. He undertook this journey for his own benefit and for the benefit of all humankind.

The Seeker

The former prince became an itinerant monk, studying under the sages of the orthodox beliefs of his day, which we would call Hinduism. He learned yogic arts and the principles of deep meditation from these teachers; he accepted their doctrine that the body was an enemy to spiritual advancement and followed their instructions concerning the best ways to curb or overcome its desires. Eventually, he became a sage in his own right—known as Sakyamuni—and set out on his own, accompanied by five followers who were similarly devoted to rigorous austerity in the pursuit of spiritual advancement. He followed this path for six long years but eventually concluded (as he approached the brink of death) that asceticism was not the road to true awareness. He began to eat and drink as he had before. His followers saw this as an admission of failure and abandoned him.

All alone, he continued his search. He took a seat beneath a now-famous bodhi tree and resolved not to move until he had attained the liberation he sought. There beneath the bodhi tree, under a full moon, his mind calmed and all became clear. He reached a point where he understood the causes of human suffering, the cycles of life and death, and all the other dilemmas that had so vexed him. At this point, he became the Buddha.

He meditated beneath the tree for a long time, and considered simply staying there—but eventually decided, out of compassion for humanity, to devote the remainder of his life to sharing what he had discovered with other seekers. Now thirty-five, he would become a teacher who showed the way of enlightenment to others.

SPIRITUALLY SPEAKING

"In Hinduism, attaining the highest life is a process of removing the bodily distractions from life, allowing one to eventually understand the Brahma nature within. In Buddhism, one follows a disciplined life to . . . understand that nothing in ourselves is 'me,' such that we dispel the very illusion of existence. In so doing, one realizes Nirvana."

—*Post on Diffen's "Compare Anything" site at diffen.com*

The Teacher

For years, he walked and preached, walked and preached, walked and preached. Unlike the elite priests of his day, the Buddha taught in the local tongues and welcomed followers from all castes, even the detested untouchables. He taught both men and women, and welcomed orders of monks and, eventually, nuns. Through it all, he rejected the doctrine of asceticism, the notion of starving oneself or otherwise punishing the body as the avenue to spiritual awakening. His philosophy was meant for all: rich, poor, young, old, male, female. He preached a committed pursuit of a personal spiritual awakening. He had no use for social hierarchies and ridiculed priests who claimed special status for themselves. He taught meditation. He embraced a path of moderation between the extremes of self-indulgence and self-denial. And he insisted that liberation is possible for any being, at any time.

CAREFUL! *Differing schools accept differing texts in this faith system. No single text unites Buddhism. The Buddha wrote no book (all the teachings attributed to him were set down long after his death), and he sought no position of formal authority.*

At the age of eighty, after he became the most revered sage in India, he lay on his side and asked his followers to pose questions. Saddened by the knowledge that his death was imminent, they could ask him nothing. Before he breathed his last, we are told, he shared with his followers these final words: "All composite things decay. Earnestly strive for your own salvation."

The Story of the Faith

If the core of the Buddha's story is single-mindedness, the core of Buddhism after his passing may well be its polar opposite: diversity. There was, is, and seems likely to be for the foreseeable future, considerable disagreement about what constitutes "authentic" Buddhism. Different groups have sharply differing conceptions of what it means to be a Buddhist.

Over two and a half millennia, Buddhism has expressed itself through any number of competing schools, and has had countless squabbles over doctrine and practice. Some of these disagreements occurred during the lifetime of the Buddha himself.

Despite, or perhaps because of, the varying interpretations, the geographic reach of the faith has been impressive and distinctive. After early propagation in India, different sects spread Buddhist doctrines to northern and southern Asia; today, it is strongly associated with the cultures of China, Tibet, Japan, Korea, and other Asian nations, and it has found an audience in Europe and North America in recent years. Buddhism in India today is a tiny tile in a vast mosaic of religions.

Three major branches of this religious tradition have sought to answer the question, "What is Buddhism?" We'll look briefly here at all three, but it must also be noted that representatives of all three have insisted that their story is the only authentic one.

The Theravada Story

Theravada means "Doctrine of the Elders." The name reflects this school's scriptural reliance on the Pali canon, which is acknowledged by most experts as the earliest record of the teachings of the Buddha. It emerged from a schism dating to about the fourth century BCE.

The Theravada school is the oldest surviving identifiable branch of Buddhist practice. It has been the dominant mode of religious expression in Sri Lanka and much of Southeast Asia for many centuries and has something like 150 million followers worldwide. The school is notable for its emphasis on "sudden awareness," in which the seeker's impurities are resolved all at once. The Theravada school is also known for aspiration toward the status of the *arhat*, a saintlike figure who is released from the cycle of birth and death.

Many adherents of the Theravada schools accept a pantheon similar to the Hindu pantheon. This sect of Buddhism has been called both pantheistic and atheistic.

Timeline of Buddhism

- **Somewhere between 566 and 490 BCE** — Gautama Siddhārtha born in Nepal.
- **Circa 405 BCE** — First Buddhist Council (Rajagrha).
- **Circa 350 BCE** — Second Buddhist Council (Vaishali).
- **Circa 250 BCE** — Third Buddhist council; schism; emergence of Theravada and Mahayana Buddhism.
- **First century BCE** — Theravada Buddhist texts compiled and formalized in Sri Lanka.
- **First century CE** — Indian Buddhists establish a presence in Southeast Asia.
- **Fourth century CE** — Vajrayana Buddhism emerges.
- **350–650 CE** — During the Gupta dynasty in India, Buddhist art and philosophy are prominent.
- **372 CE** — Buddhism present in Korea.
- **Circa 600–650 CE** — Vajrayana Buddhism established in Tibet.
- **618–907 CE** — Golden Age of Chinese Buddhism.
- **836–842 CE** — Tibetan emperor persecutes Buddhists there.
- **845 CE** — Chinese officials begin official suppression of Buddhism there.
- **Early 10th century CE** — Korea formulates a Buddhist constitution.
- **Mid-twelfth century** — Buddhism has all but vanished from India.

1578 CE	Sonam Gyatso named the Dalai Lama by Altan Khan.
1617 CE	Establishment of rule of Tibet by Dalai Lamas.
1891 CE	Buddhist revival movement begins in India.
1949 CE	Official Chinese Communist campaign against Tibetan Buddhists begins.

KEY TERMS DEMYSTIFIED: Theism Debate, Theravada Buddhists, and Mahayana

A **theism debate** within Buddhism concerns the nature of the Buddha and reflects a divide that touches on questions of worship and divinity. **Theravada Buddhists** consider the Buddha a human who, through human striving, attained nirvana, a state beyond suffering; some Buddhists from the **Mahayana** school, on the other hand, believe the Buddha to embody a cosmic "inconceivable" aspect of being and to have been born for the benefit of other beings. In addition, some Mahayana schools worship a saintlike enlightened being known as Avalokitesvara.

The Mahayana Story

Mahayana translates as "great vehicle." This is the dominant form of Buddhism in northern Asia; it also arose as a response to the religious disputes that emerged centuries after the death of the Buddha. Although the Mahayana school accepts the scriptures of Theravada Buddhism, it adds its own tidal wave of devotional and philosophical texts, notably the Mahayana sutras. This strain of Buddhism also presents for the devotee a figure distinctive to Mahayana traditions: the bodhisattva, about whom we will learn more in the next chapter.

Mahayana Buddhism is notable for its ability to absorb and refine local cultures into its practices. As a result, Mahayana Buddhism has often expressed itself quite differently in different parts of the world. Among the most influential and enduring of those expressions has been Zen Buddhism, a school prominent in China, Japan, and Korea (and later in other parts of the world) that emphasized direct experience. Realization of one's inherent Buddha-nature is emphasized over the study of religious texts or participation in elaborate rituals.

Zen does not do away entirely with texts and rituals—over the centuries, it has acquired plenty of both—but it does subsume them within the context of a personal relationship with a Zen master and the practice of meditation. Zen's emphasis on authenticity, self-control, and discipline has made it one of the most influential schools in all of Buddhism.

SPIRITUALLY SPEAKING

"Zen includes the wide diversity of the Buddhist pantheon, but also teaches that the divine nature is in all things and that the Buddha-nature is shared by everyone. There is no concept of omnipotent, eternal deities."

—*Post on Patheos.com, "Hosting Conversations on Faith"*

The Vajrayana Story

Vajrayana Buddhism is also known as Tibetan Buddhism and Diamond Vehicle Buddhism. It is thought to have arisen in India in the sixth or seventh century BCE—perhaps a thousand years after the passing of the Buddha. Believers hold, however, that this school's doctrines are in fact directly traceable to a tradition of secret teachings attributable directly to the Buddha. The claim is fraught with controversy, but that controversy appears to have had little effect on the influence of this strand of the Buddhist faith. The main scriptures of Vajrayana Buddhism are called Tantras.

The Vajrayana school of Buddhism is today perhaps most strongly identified with the Dalai Lama, a figure believed by devotees of the Gelug or "Yellow Hat" sect to be the latest rebirth of the figure known as Avalokitesvara. This Avalokitesvara is believed to be a repeatedly reincarnated leader who compassionately accepts rebirth in order to bring others to enlightenment. Because of the Dalai Lama's traditional role as political leader in Tibet, the current (fourteenth) Dalai Lama has encountered opposition from the present government of China, which opposes both Tibetan independence and expressions of Tibetan religious faith.

The Buddha wrote no book (all the teachings attributed to him were set down long after his death), and he sought no position of formal authority.

Summary

- The Buddha is regarded as one of the most influential figures in human history. Traditionally, his final teaching was "All composite things decay. Earnestly strive for your own salvation."

- *Theravada* means "Doctrine of the Elders." This school relies on the Pali Canon, which is acknowledged by most experts as the earliest record of the teachings of the Buddha.

- *Mahayana* translates as "great vehicle." This is the dominant form of Buddhism in northern Asia; it arose as a response to religious disputes centuries after the death of the Buddha.

- The Vajrayana school of Buddhism is identified with the Dalai Lama, a figure believed by devotees of the Gelug or "Yellow Hat" sect to be the latest rebirth of Avalokitesvara.

QUIZ

1. **We believe that the figure who eventually became known as the Buddha began life as a prince in**
   A. China.
   B. Tibet.
   C. Nepal.
   D. None of the above.

2. **Buddhism is notable for its rejection of**
   A. asceticism.
   B. meditation.
   C. preaching.
   D. None of the above.

3. **Practitioners of Theravada Buddhism are now likely to be found in**
   A. China.
   B. Australia.
   C. Sri Lanka.
   D. None of the above.

4. **The Dalai Lama is**
   A. a Theravada Buddhist.
   B. a Mahayana Buddhist.
   C. a Vajrayana Buddhist.
   D. None of the above.

5. **The Buddha personally wrote**
   A. the Diamond Sutra.
   B. no book.
   C. a catechism for early Buddhists.
   D. None of the above.

6. The person whose dying words were "All composite things decay. Earnestly strive for your own salvation" was

   A. the Dalai Lama.

   B. the Buddha.

   C. an unidentified Zen master.

   D. None of the above.

7. After its early propagation in India, Buddhism is today strongly associated with the cultures of

   A. China, Tibet, Japan, Korea, and other Asian nations.

   B. the countries of North and South America.

   C. Indonesia and West Africa.

   D. None of the above.

8. Many adherents of the Theravada schools of Buddhism accept

   A. a pantheon similar to the Norse pantheon.

   B. a pantheon similar to the Hindu pantheon.

   C. a pantheon similar to the Greek pantheon.

   D. None of the above.

9. True or false: Mahayana Buddhism is notable for its ability to absorb and refine local cultures into its practices.

10. The practice of Zen Buddhism emphasizes

   A. direct experience.

   B. ritual animal sacrifice.

   C. formal denunciation of the Eightfold Path.

   D. None of the above.

Chapter **4**

Buddhism: Core Beliefs and Practices

There are something like 300 million Buddhists on earth. When you complete this chapter, you will be able to describe some of the most important beliefs and practices within contemporary Buddhism.

CHAPTER OBJECTIVES

In this chapter, you will learn about:

- What Buddhists believe about reincarnation
- The Buddhist conception of karma
- The different types of karma
- The Four Noble Truths
- The Six Realms
- The Five Precepts
- The precepts Buddhist monks follow
- Samsara
- The Eightfold Path

We'll begin with the subject that has, perhaps, attracted the most attention from people outside the faith.

Reincarnation

One of the best known and most discussed of Buddhism's core beliefs is the foundational concept that it shares with Hinduism, the faith system from which it emerged: the concept of reincarnation.

Buddhists believe that at the death of one personality, a new one comes into being, much as the flame of a dying candle can serve to light the flame of another. The consciousness in the new person is neither equal to nor entirely dissimilar from that in the departed, but the two form a causal continuum or stream.

Unlike Judaism, Islam, and Christianity (to give only three of the most obvious examples), the Buddhist thought system assumes that we go through not one, but many cycles of birth, life, death, and rebirth. It assumes that our attainment of true spiritual freedom, our true awakening, is synonymous with our liberation from the cycle of birth and death—and from the delusion that our identity is somehow separate from that of the created universe.

CAREFUL! *An important cautionary note is in order here. Buddhist notions of physical rebirth have to be understood in the context of the Buddha's own teachings about the transitory nature of all existence. These teachings create distinctly Buddhist chords of doctrine and belief on (among other things) reincarnation, beliefs that sometimes resonate very differently from Hinduism's.*

There are, of course, similarities between Buddhism and Hinduism when it comes to reincarnation. One strong parallel with Hinduism's doctrines is the Buddhist idea that a sequence of lives play out, one after another, over an extended period of time. In Buddhist belief, however, there is no consistent, indivisible self that unites the consciousness of these physical bodies, or the viewpoints that experience the rebirths.

According to the Buddhists, the human perspective and personality, like everything else, is subject to being dissolved and even recombined with other elements. Thus, in the Buddhist system of thought, the process of rebirth may express itself with an incarnation in any of many states of being, including human, animal, and various types of supernatural entities. This system of rebirth is consistent with the Buddhist doctrine of the Six Realms.

Reincarnation and the Six Realms

In classical Buddhist doctrine, beings are reborn into one of six realms of existence. The realm you are reincarnated into is determined by your karma. (Buddhism's conception of karma differs slightly from Hinduism's, as we shall see.) All of these realms are impermanent and imperfect, a concept known in this tradition as *dukkha*. These realms show some of Buddhism's most overt overlapping with the structures of Hinduism.

- **Deva-gati.** The first realm in Buddhist doctrine is Deva-gati, or more simply the realm of the Gods. This is the home of beings who are the most privileged, possess power over others, and enjoy wealth. However, these beings are limited by the inability to recognize suffering in others and are deprived of compassion. These faults lead to total lack of wisdom despite their luxuries.
- **Asura-gati.** This second realm is inhabited by beings of great strength and jealousy. Existing as demigods, these beings are preoccupied by materialism and the desire to compete and overcome enemies, especially Devas. Many scholars compare these titans to human beings since both struggle with the forces of good and evil in their actions.
- **Preta-gati.** Known as the realm of the hungry ghost, here is where the demons of consumerism are illustrated most starkly. These beings are characterized by their inability to satisfy their greed and cravings with huge empty stomachs and tiny mouths. They suffer with eternal starvation because their desires never end. Humans who are covetous and shallow often are reincarnated into these beings and suffer in this realm.
- **Naraka-gati.** The realm of hell, Naraka-gati is the darkest and most painful of the six realms. It is populated by demon beings who are driven solely by anger and act only in terms of violence. Incapable of knowing love, they attack any being that shows them compassion and drive away others. They're only capable of coexisting with other hell beings. A human life driven by aggression can lead to a life in this hell and constant torture. Escape from this realm is possible when all of the stored negative karma is exhausted.
- **Tiryagyoni-gati.** This is known as the animal realm and is one of the hardest cycles of karma to escape. It is an existence marked by ignorance, blind subservience, and laziness. This realm is especially difficult to escape because beings that possess a combination of stupidity and complacency tend to remain in that condition. This realm often interacts with the sixth and final realm of the human, much like the realms of the Devas and the titans are intertwined and codependent.

- **Manusya-gati.** This final realm, the human, is the only realm from which an escape from samsara, the potentially endless cycle of rebirth into one or more of these six realms, is possible. (We will define samsara using more detail in the next section.) If you are a being who is characterized by passion, doubt, and desire, you are incarnated as a human. As a human, your goal is to achieve enlightenment and escape samsara. Like the titans in their realm, humans have a capacity for both good and evil, and while humans alone have the ability to achieve enlightenment, very few will reach it.

In Buddhist cosmology, these six realms are divided by their placement in three different levels:

- Heaven
- Earth
- Hell

Devi and Asura occupy the level of heaven, with Devi at the higher aspect and Asura at the lower aspect; animals and humans occupy the earth, with the humans above the animals as a result of the human ability to achieve enlightenment. Finally, hell is the level of the demons in the fourth realm. The "hungry ghosts" can travel in the realms of heaven and hell but are incapable of interacting with any of the beings that exist there. They are confined by their desires.

Samsara

An understanding of the concept of *samsara* is necessary at this point. It can be defined many different ways, but most simply put it is the potentially endless cycle of suffering that all living beings experience.

> ## KEY TERMS DEMYSTIFIED: **Samsara**
>
> One translation from Sanskrit to English defines **samsara** as "continuous movement." The goal of Buddhism in its most basic essence is to find an escape from this powerful cycle of life, death, and rebirth.

Escape from this cycle is made possible by the Four Noble Truths. We'll get to them in a little bit.

Before that, though, it's important to understand that samsara is a process and not a physical state. Each being is subject to his or her own samsara; each being creates a world for each reincarnation as he or she sees fit.

This world is usually filled with various states of suffering brought by the feelings of desire, greed, envy, and anger, to name a few. Upon the conclusion of this world, the being transmigrates to another world he or she can then create. This cycle is seemingly endless until the being reaches a state of enlightenment and moves beyond feelings of desire and enters the journey into Nirvana. Thus, samsara is the antithesis of Nirvana. Suffering of each being in the cycle of samsara has gone on for an inconceivable amount of time.

SPIRITUALLY SPEAKING

"The Buddha once asked his monks, 'Which do you think is greater: the water in the oceans or the tears you've shed while wandering on [though samsara]?' His answer: the tears."

—*Famous fable of samsara, derived from Thanissaro Bhikkhu, an American Buddhist monk*

Karma, Revisited

Within the Buddhist system of thought (as distinct from Hinduism), reincarnation is best understood as a *collective* undertaking by which *all* sentient life strives for liberation from ignorance.

Rebirth is affected by the karmas (mental, physical, and verbal actions) of past lives, with good karmas producing a more favorable rebirth and bad karmas delivering one that is less favorable. The cycle continues, Buddhists believe, as long as our consciousness remains bogged down in ignorance. When, after many cycles of life, we free ourselves from ignorance, the cycle of rebirth ends, our karma is resolved, suffering ends, and we attain a state known as Nirvana.

Recall that *karma* means "action" or "doing"—a course of cause and effect. From the Buddhist perspective, inequalities can be explained in two ways:

either they are purely coincidental and arise from randomness, or they are an effect of causation. Or, to look at it another way: some inequality or apparent injustice could not reasonably be seen as caused by the chaos of nature, so there must be another factor causing inequalities among living beings. This factor is karma.

Broadly speaking, Buddhists believe that each being's actions result from his or her internal feelings, emotions, and thoughts. Therefore, the consequences of each action are justified by that person's actions.

Different Types of Karma

Functional karma is classified into four kinds within Buddhism: reproductive, supportive, obstructive, and destructive.

Reproductive Karma

Buddhists believe that every birth is determined by a past good or bad karma that dominates at the moment of death. Karma that determines the future birth is called reproductive karma. It is this last thought that determines the state of a person in his or her following birth. This is either good or bad karma.

The gender of a person is decided at the very beginning of a being. It is conditioned by karma and is not a random combination of sperm and ovum cells. The suffering and joy one experiences in the course of one's lifetime are, similarly, an unavoidable result of reproductive karma in Buddhist thought.

Supportive Karma

Supportive karma comes near reproductive karma and supports it. It is neither good nor bad, and it helps or preserves the action of the reproductive karma during one's lifetime. Immediately after conception until the moment of death, this karma supports reproductive karma.

Buddhists believe that a moral supportive karma helps in giving health, wealth, happiness, and so on to the being born with a moral reproductive karma. An immoral supportive karma, on the other hand, assists in giving pain, sorrow, and other such experiences to the being born with an immoral reproductive karma.

Obstructive Karma or Counteractive Karma

Obstructive karma deteriorates, disrupts, and impedes the fulfillment of the reproductive karma. For example, a person born with a good reproductive karma might have assorted ailments that prevent him from enjoying the benefits of his good actions. However, an animal that is born with a bad reproductive karma may lead a comfortable life as a result of his good obstructive karma preventing the execution of the bad reproductive karma.

Destructive Karma

In Buddhism, the law of karma says that the potential energy of the reproductive karma could be reversed by a more dominant opposing karma of the past. Destructive karma is more efficient than obstructive or supportive karma as it doesn't just block the force of karma, but obliterates it. Think about an arrow that is shot but falls to the ground because of some powerful obstruction in its path. The obstruction can be good or it can be bad.

For example, tradition holds that all four karmas activated within the life of Devadatta. He was the cousin and the brother-in-law of Buddha himself. He was a good Buddhist monk who eventually became conceited and arrogant due to his popularity. He became jealous of Buddha and executed many failed plots to kill him. When those didn't work, he tried to discredit Buddha and make a rift between Buddha and his disciples so that they would follow Devadatta instead.

Karma: Putting It All Together

Let's consider that example closely. Devadatta had good reproductive karma because he was born into a royal family. His supportive karma gave him easy wealth and fame. His destructive karma led to the jealousy and the negative behavior toward the Buddha. Obstructive karma blocked the good karma when he contracted an illness that slowly killed him. By the time of his death, he was sincerely repentant for his actions, but it was too late. He wished to see the Buddha before he died, but the labor of his evil karma had come to fruition and prevented the fulfillment of that wish. Destructive karma caused him to become more and more ill on his way to see the Buddha, and he died near the gate of the monastery where the Buddha was staying.

Nirvana

Centuries before it was the name of a rock and roll band, Nirvana was a term famous for its association with Buddhism—and equally famous, perhaps, for its difficulty to define. One popular answer to the question, "What is Nirvana?" sounds like this: "A beam of light that never lands anywhere." There are many other answers to consider, many of which involve prayerful meditation.

A Buddhist prayer wheel. Prayer is an example of Right Action, part of Buddhism's Eightfold Path.

Credit: Purestock/SuperStock

SPIRITUALLY SPEAKING

"Someone who has set out in the vehicle of a Bodhisattva should decide that 'I must lead all the beings to Nirvana, into that realm of Nirvana which leaves nothing behind.' What is this realm of Nirvana which leaves nothing behind?"

—*The Buddha*

KEY TERMS DEMYSTIFIED: Bodhisattva

Generally understood by Buddhists to be an enlightened being who is able to reach Nirvana, but who forgoes it in order to save suffering beings.

The Four Noble Truths

Of great importance within Buddhism are the core precepts known as the Four Noble Truths of the Buddha. These four concepts examine the source and the remedy for human suffering. Often oversimplified, they are nevertheless important starting points for the newcomer, initial ideas that can be explored in their fuller dimensions after one has gotten a good grasp on the basics of this extremely broad and rich faith system.

A "for beginners" summary of the Four Noble Truths follows. Notice that each Noble Truth is expressed in a single word that carries within it vast reservoirs of meaning.

- **Dukkha.** Suffering exists. It is a nonnegotiable part of our existence and can even be considered universal. To be part of the cycle of birth, death, and rebirth is to experience suffering.
- **Samudaya.** Suffering has causes. Among these are desire, anger, and ignorance—three major categories that can be broken down into subcauses like the urge to possess and control, the insistence on being right, obsession with sensuality, and so on.

- **Nirodha.** Suffering has an end. Upon experiencing Nirvana, the final liberation, the mind becomes clear, experiences total freedom, and is freed from all attachment and delusion. Desire, anger, and ignorance are no longer hindrances.
- **Magga.** To end suffering, follow the Eightfold Path. This is where Buddhists move (as it were) from theory to practice. (A summary appears in the next section.)

Taken together, these principles are regarded by Buddhists as superior, accessible, nondeceptive instructions of benefit to all humankind.

SPIRITUALLY SPEAKING

"You should know sufferings.
You should abandon origins.
You should attain cessations.
You should practice the path."

—*The Buddha, "Sutra of the Four Noble Truths"*

The Eightfold Path

Buddhism stands in contrast to other faiths for many reasons, and here we come to one of the most striking. For the Eightfold Path—the subject of the fourth of the four great truths of this faith, and the doctrinal heart of Buddhism—is a process, not a set of rules.

Its purpose is to help the Buddhist practitioner transcend and overcome delusions and conditioned responses that obscure his or her true Buddha-nature. The Eightfold Path is more about releasing misconceptions and discarding one's own unhelpful reactions than it is about learning, obeying, or achieving anything. In this sense, Buddhism offers an approach that many consider pragmatic and accessible, focused less on concepts like reconciliation or sin and more on the progress of the individual believer.

The teachings embodied within the Eightfold Path are known as *upaya*, which translates roughly as "expedient method." They are meant to be useful, and are best thought of as tools rather than dogma.

The eight components of the Buddhist path are:

1. **Right Vision**, meaning a complete and unencumbered understanding of reality and of the changing nature of existence.

2. **Right Aspiration**, meaning an attitude or thought process that allows the believer to respond to all situations from a place of compassion and love.

3. **Right Speech**, meaning communication that is honest, upright, and without malicious intent.

4. **Right Action**, meaning action based on respect for life and the desire to avoid exploitation, in accordance with the Five Precepts (see next section).

5. **Right Livelihood**, meaning a life whose economics—personal and social—are based on principles of ethical, respectful action that exploits no participant.

6. **Right Effort**, meaning the ability to focus one's life energy diligently, creatively, and constructively.

7. **Right Mindfulness**, meaning the ability to cultivate and maintain a balanced awareness of oneself, one's surroundings, other creatures and organisms, and the universe at large.

8. **Right Meditation**, meaning complete concentration (samadhi)—and, ultimately, the liberated state known as Buddhahood or enlightenment.

Notice that each of these is (or at least can be) a present-tense principle of action—a process or direction—rather than a rigid standard or ideal for "good" or "bad" behavior.

KEY TERMS DEMYSTIFIED: **Samadhi**

A level of concentrated meditation that can be described as a state of consciousness in which the consciousness of the observer becomes one with the consciousness of that which is observed.

SPIRITUALLY SPEAKING

"Laya Samadhi begins in intense meditation and manifests as a wellspring of joy akin to that experienced during dancing or singing. In Savikalpa Samadhi, the meditator briefly experiences space and time in a different way. His/her imagination (kalpa) remains active and hence he/she 'sees' the myriad desires that remain unfulfilled in his/her life. In this Samadhi however, the realization comes that he/she is but an instrument in their completion. Ideas flood in, but are observed detachedly. In the third stage—Nirvikalpa Samadhi—such attachments and the actions that give rise to them (karma) dissolve. The heart ceases to beat. The meditator is filled with infinite bliss and becomes both the object of joy and the one who rejoices. There is a sense of tremendous power accompanied by the sensation of containing the universe within. . . . Emerging from Nirvikalpa Samadhi, one may not recall his/her name or communicate normally and may experience reluctance to return to functioning like an ordinary human being. Sahaja Samadhi is the supreme level of meditation where the meditator attains the highest levels of consciousness yet is able to function effectively in the material world. Such an individual has conquered reality, a rare feat. To experience Sahaja Samadhi, it is necessary to become one with the divine."

—*Post on BuddhaGroove.Net*

The Five Precepts

Buddhism promotes five basic guidelines by which to live. Its list of five precepts is reminiscent of similar rules that can be found in the Ten Commandments of Judaism and Christianity. Such comparisons are common and perhaps helpful. It's important to note, however, that the Five Precepts are recommendations, not inviolable rules. Individual Buddhists are meant to use their own discretion and experience in determining exactly how to implement these five guidelines. The Five Precepts are as follows:

1. Do not kill. Sometimes translated as "do not harm," this precept promotes nonviolence, which is regarded as a core tenet of Buddhism.

2. Do not steal.

3. Do not lie.

4. Do not misuse sex.

5. Do not consume intoxicants.

There are other precepts as well. Precepts 6 through 10 are observed by Buddhists in preparation for monastic life and by devoted laypeople without familial attachments. (Laypeople may observe the first eight precepts on Buddhist festival days.)

6. Do not eat food between noon and dawn.

7. Do not dance, sing, listen to music, or watch grotesque mime.

8. Do not use garlands, perfumes, and personal adornment.

9. Do not sit in places located on a higher level than the noble beings.

10. Do not accept gold or silver.

In addition, there are numerous specific rules of conduct that Buddhist monks (*bhikkhus*) are obliged to observe.

Buddhism in a Box	
Divinity	A point of dispute. See "Key Terms Demystified: Theism Debate" in Chapter 3.
Afterlife	After death, one is either transmigrated into another body or one goes to Nirvana. Transmigration is rebirth. *Nirvana* literally means "to extinguish." It is the final conclusion of the cycle of death and rebirth.
Purpose of Human Life	One must be aware that forming attachments or longings for material things and for people will cause sorrow. Karma from previous lives may cause the attachment. Detaching from these things, by recognizing their fleetingness or the karma will decrease suffering. This will free oneself from greed, envy, and delusion, making Nirvana a closer possibility.
Distinctive Practices and Beliefs	Buddhists who are not monks are encouraged to meditate, to chant or to copy sutras, to donate to monks or monasteries, and to perform good deeds that could lead to a more desirable rebirth. Some Buddhists use amulets for protection from demons. The Four Noble Truths form the foundation of belief for all branches of Buddhism.
Outsiders Often Distracted by	The doctrine of nonattachment, which is often mistaken for the belief that Buddhists hate life, promote nihilism, and so on.

Summary

- Buddhists believe that at the death of one personality, a new one comes into being. In the Buddhist doctrine of reincarnation, beings are reborn into one of six realms of existence.

- There are different kinds of karma in Buddhist thought.

- One popular answer to the question, "What is Nirvana?" is "A beam of light that never lands anywhere."

- In Buddhist thought, the Four Noble Truths examine the source and remedy for human suffering.

- The Eightfold Path—the subject of the fourth of the Four Noble Truths, and the doctrinal heart of Buddhism—is a process, not a set of rules.

- Individual Buddhists are meant to use their own discretion and experience in determining exactly how to implement the Five Precepts.

QUIZ

1. **"Bodhisattva" is best defined as**
   A. a modern innovation found only in twenty-first-century Buddhism.
   B. an enlightened being who is able to reach Nirvana, but who forgoes it in order to save suffering beings.
   C. a "hungry ghost."
   D. None of the above.

2. **Right Meditation is an element of**
   A. the Eightfold Path.
   B. the Four Noble Truths.
   C. the Five Precepts.
   D. None of the above.

3. **Dukkha, the notion that "suffering exists," is an element of**
   A. the Eightfold Path.
   B. the Four Noble Truths.
   C. the Five Precepts.
   D. None of the above.

4. **The injunction not to kill is an element of**
   A. the Eightfold Path.
   B. the Four Noble Truths.
   C. the Five Precepts.
   D. none of the above.

5. **The injunction not to accept gold or silver is an element of**
   A. the Eightfold Path.
   B. the Four Noble Truths.
   C. the Five Precepts.
   D. None of the above.

6. **Samadhi is**
   A. a city in Nepal.
   B. one of the Five Precepts.
   C. a level of concentrated meditation that can be described as a state of consciousness in which the consciousness of the observer becomes one with the consciousness of that which is observed.
   D. None of the above.

7. **The Five Precepts include the guidance**
   A. to convert others to Buddhism.
   B. not to eat seafood.
   C. not to wear silk.
   D. None of the above.

8. **True or false: Buddhism and Hinduism share identical teachings on reincarnation.**

9. **True or false: There are no Buddhist monks.**

10. **Buddhists believe that consciously forming attachments or longings for material things and/or people will**
    A. lead to a state of spiritual fulfillment.
    B. lead to sorrow.
    C. honor and fulfill the teachings of Buddha.
    D. None of the above.

chapter **5**

Taoism: History and Context

Taoism is an ancient, important, and highly influential belief system. Upon completing this chapter, you will be able to explain its origins and development.

In this chapter, you will learn about:

- What the Tao is
- The debate over the definition of Taoism
- Taoism's emergence
- The most important Taoist texts
- The authorship of those texts

The big debate about Taoism (pronounced DOW-ism) is whether or not to call it a religion in the first place. Is it a philosophical movement? A code of ethics? And what is the Tao, anyway?

KEY TERMS DEMYSTIFIED: Tao

The fundamental principle underlying the universe, "the way things are." This one word, endlessly influential in Oriental thought and religious practice, combines within itself the complementary principles of yin (female, negative, dark) and yang (male, positive, bright) energy—and also identifies the Way, or code of behavior, that harmoniously aligns with the natural order of things.

The yin-yang symbol.
Credit: © Photodisc/Getty Images

So: Is Taoism a religion? The safest way through this much-debated question is to label Taoism a vitally important "religious and philosophical tradition." That means to accept from the outset that Taoism has influenced people in a manner very different from that of the other religions described in this book. It brings the beauty and elegance of philosophical "first principles" to the discussion of human meaning, behavior, and purpose. This is the best way to grasp Taoism's unique, seemingly ageless appeal.

We can begin our examination of this belief system by acknowledging the unique corner of the devotional spectrum it has managed to create for itself. Once we get a sense of what makes Taoism so distinctive, the history will make a little more sense.

The Big Idea

There was no social framework, no list of mandatory duties, no sins to avoid, no hierarchy either demanded or implied in the earliest expressions of what we now call Taoism. There were no monastic orders, no priests, no rituals, and no institutions. There were no codes of conduct, no commandments, no way to join the faith, and no way to be excommunicated from it. There was, in fact, no faith to join.

What there was, was teaching focused on the Tao.

Eventually, Taoism attracted many of the trappings of more conventional religious structures. But the early teachings that form the foundation of that structure arose from not one but two extraordinary sources, sources that appear to have developed independently from one another. This teaching preceded any of the formal "religious" elements that later emerged, elements we are inclined to think of as essential components of any religious practice.

This is why you hear so many people insist that Taoism is, at its root, not so much a religious system as a philosophy. Whatever you call it, it is rooted in a single powerful idea. That idea has proved so profound, so beautiful, so enduring, and so influential over time that it has proved difficult for many people not to want to trace it to something eternal. The so-called "big idea" of Taoism is this:

> The universe operates harmoniously according to its own ways. Whenever we exert our independent will against those ways, or use it to divide the world into artificial categories, we disrupt that harmony.

Where other faith systems may set out specific actions and narrowly defined codes of conduct, the classic Taoist texts are more likely to counsel skepticism and applaud the willingness to do nothing and want nothing. A famous Taoist question asks the human being whether he or she has the patience to wait until the mud settles and the water is clear. This is the basic stance of Taoism: patience, passivity, openness, emptiness. The stance is captured within the important Chinese word *wu-wei*. Taoism's history, outlook, and influence are more or less meaningless without it.

> ## KEY TERMS DEMYSTIFIED: Wu-wei
>
> A central concept in Taoism that literally means "nonaction" or "nondoing." The principle has also been rendered as *wei-wu-wei*, meaning "action without actions." A flower that grows, a river that flows, a planet that orbits—all of these phenomena take place in the natural order of things, without conscious effort. Human activity can benefit, Taoists maintain, by imitating such examples.

Taoism's Two Main Textual Sources

In this chapter, we'll look at the two great early textual sources that originally expressed and consolidated this "big Taoist idea." The basic concepts—or perhaps the better word is *perspectives*—of Taoism are set out in these two extraordinary, elusive books. They established a practical and eloquent means of looking at life, society, and the individual's place in the world. One "official" expression of Taoism became the state religion in China for a time, beginning in the seventh century of the Common Era, before eventually losing ground to Confucianism. Taoism remained a vitally important part of Chinese culture, however, and the core concepts of its two scriptures began to merge with a variety of Chinese folk traditions.

As a result, the teachings of these two books have resounded into virtually all corners of Asian (and, for that matter, non-Asian) society. They continue to serve as the foundation for a vast array of customs, schools, and practices in China and elsewhere.

SPIRITUALLY SPEAKING

"According to the Taoists, yang and yin, light and shadow, useful and useless are all different aspects of the whole, and the minute we choose one side and block out the other, we upset nature's balance. If we are to be whole and follow the way of nature, we must pursue the difficult process of embracing the opposites."

—*Connie Zweig*,
Meeting the Shadow:
The Hidden Power of the Dark Side of Human Nature

The *Tao Te Ching*

At least four centuries before the birth of Christ, and perhaps as long ago as six centuries before that event, the shortest, most ambiguous of all sacred texts emerged in China. It was, and is, known as the *Tao Te Ching* (also spelled *Daodejing* or *Dao De Jing*), a phrase that can be translated in any number of ways, but that I will render as "The Great Book of the Way and the Power."

The text is traditionally attributed to a sage known as Lao-tzu, whose historical existence (unlike the Buddha's) is a matter of intense scholarly debate. Whether he existed as an independent thinker or as a fictional figure who serves as a composite of ancient teachers, Lao-tzu's influence on world affairs has been substantial. The book's 5,000 or so Chinese characters, broken up into eighty-one concise chapters, have been among the most constantly repeated, translated, and cited words in human history. Its insights and advice have been deeply woven into Chinese culture for millennia.

The book is ambiguous, engaging, and brilliant. Its content depends largely on the situation and perspective of the reader and can range from shrewd political advice for powerful rulers to practical insights on the day-to-day struggles faced by those in the humblest stations of life. The *Tao Te Ching* consists of a sequence of very brief poems that can be, and have been, interpreted in countless ways, but whose main themes include the idea that the Tao—which I translate as "the Way"—transcends human naming and distinctions, precedes notions of time and space, and supports and sustains the entire universe. Throughout the text, themes of balance, emptiness, and openness to the guidance, creative capacity, and restorative force of the Way resonate powerfully.

The claim that the *Tao Te Ching* is "only" a philosophical treatise becomes (for some) difficult to maintain once one has read its seemingly all-encompassing opening passage:

> The tao that can be described
> is not the eternal Tao.
> The name that can be spoken
> is not the eternal Name.
>
> The nameless is the boundary of Heaven and Earth.
> The named is the mother of creation.

Freed from desire, you can see the hidden mystery.
By having desire, you can only see what is visibly real.

Yet mystery and reality
emerge from the same source.
This source is called darkness.

Darkness born from darkness.
The beginning of all understanding.

Another famous passage reads:

Knowing you don't know is wholeness.
Thinking you know is a disease.
Only by recognizing that you have an illness
can you move to seek a cure.

The Master is whole because
she sees her illnesses and treats them,
and thus is able to remain whole.

Another classic passage on emptiness advises as follows:

Thirty spokes are joined together in a wheel,
but it is the center hole
that allows the wheel to function.

We mold clay into a pot,
but it is the emptiness inside
that makes the vessel useful.

We fashion wood for a house,
but it is the emptiness inside
that makes it livable.

We work with the substantial,
but the emptiness is what we use.

The massive influence of this tiny, ancient book on Chinese culture and tradition
(and particularly on Chinese Buddhism and Confucianism) is hard to overstate.

It has been endlessly interpreted, reinterpreted, and adapted to fit innumerable political and social demands. In addition to being the shortest, it may be the most flexible religious scripture in human history. It has, down the centuries, inspired essays on topics as diverse as the ethics of political leadership, effective military strategy, and gardening.

KEY TERMS DEMYSTIFIED: Confucianism

An important ethical and philosophical system based on the principles of the ancient Chinese philosopher Master Kong, known more commonly in the contemporary West as Confucius.

As influential as it is, the *Tao Te Ching* is not the last word on Taoism. It is one of the intriguing features of this movement that the tradition expounding the singular Way has not one, but two sacred texts—texts apparently created entirely independently of one another, but that fit each other like gears in clockwork.

The second great text of Taoism is known as the *Zhuangzi*.

CAREFUL! *The early texts of Taoism set out no clear list of forbidden or permitted behaviors. Looking for them is a mistake. What is to be found instead are the "Three Jewels" or "Three Treasures," guidelines of particular interest to social leaders. These three broad principles have been defined as Compassion, Moderation, and Humility. The scholar Arthur Waley described them as "rules that form the practical, political side" of Taoist doctrine. He connected Compassion with "abstention from aggressive war and capital punishment," Moderation with "absolute simplicity of living," and Humility with "refusal to assert active authority."*

The *Zhuangzi*

"Once upon a time, I, Zhuangzi, dreamt I was a butterfly, fluttering hither and thither, to all intents and purposes a butterfly. I was conscious only of my happiness as a butterfly, unaware that I was Zhuangzi. Soon I awoke, and there I was, veritably myself again. Now I do not know whether I was then a man dreaming I was a butterfly, or whether I am now a butterfly, dreaming I am a man. Between a man and a butterfly there is necessarily a distinction. The transition is called the transformation of material things."

—*Zhuangzi*

The *Zhuangzi* is the second foundational text of the Taoist philosophical and religious tradition. It is also the name of the author of the text. The *Zhuangzi*, which is longer than the *Tao Te Ching*, has been subject to commentary by countless philosophers, Asian and otherwise, since roughly the third century before the Common Era. Like the *Tao Te Ching*, it is timeless.

The Taoism of Zhuangzi is distinctive. It advocates an escape from the pressures of society and encourages the willingness to forge a unique personal trail of freedom and autonomy. It has been seen by many readers as encouragement to secede from social and political obligations in order to seek a private life of self-cultivation.

SPIRITUALLY SPEAKING

"Immersed in the wonder of the Tao, you can deal with whatever life brings you, and when death comes, you are ready."

—*Zhuangzi*

This point of entry to the classic themes of emptiness and openness complement the *Tao Te Ching*'s more communally focused principles, which are often interpreted as offering guidance in the difficult task of establishing sound leadership within a society. Where the *Tao Te Ching* inspires with the possibility of maintaining harmony and continuity in one's relations with other people, the *Zhuangzi* inspires with the possibility of personal authenticity.

Taoism's two core scriptures have been endlessly reassessed and reinterpreted. Here is a seventeenth-century recapitulation of the classic ancient Taoist texts by Miyamoto Musashi, a Japanese swordsman and author of *The Book of Five Rings*.

1. Accept everything as it is.

2. Don't seek pleasure for the sake of pleasure.

3. Don't depend on a partial feeling under any circumstances.

4. Think light of yourself and deep on the world.

5. Be detached from desire for your whole life.

6. Regret nothing you have done.

7. No jealousy.

8. No letting yourself be saddened by separation.

9. Resentment and complaint are inappropriate for both oneself and others.

10. Don't allow yourself to be driven by feelings of lust or love.

11. Have no preference in anything.

12. Be indifferent about where you live.

13. Don't crave the taste of good food.

14. Don't hold on to the possessions you no longer need.

15. Don't follow customary beliefs.

16. Don't collect weapons or practice with weapons beyond what is useful.

17. Don't fear death.

18. Don't seek to possess either wealth or title for your old age.

19. Respect Buddha and the gods without counting on help from them.

20. You may yield your own body (in combat), but you must preserve your honor.

21. Never stray from the Tao.

And a twenty-first-century recapitulation:

"Be desireless. Be excellent. Be gone."

—The Tao of Steve, *2001 film*

Summary

- Taoism is a massively influential religious and philosophical tradition.
- Two core texts lie at the historical heart of Taoism.
- The *Tao Te Ching*, attributed to Lao-tzu, is the world's most concise religious text.
- It is famously ambiguous, but it has been interpreted as offering timeless advice on leadership and the harmonious conduct of personal relationships.
- More personally focused is the denser, second core text of Taoism, the *Zhuangzi*.
- These two ancient scriptures established a practical means of looking at life, society, and the individual's place in the world.

QUIZ

1. **Taoism is best understood as**
   A. a solely religious tradition.
   B. a solely philosophical tradition.
   C. a religious and philosophical tradition.
   D. None of the above.

2. ***Wu-wei* means**
   A. "nondoing."
   B. "active, conscious effort."
   C. "respect for the Buddha."
   D. None of the above.

3. **The *Tao Te Ching* is**
   A. the world's shortest major religious text.
   B. the world's longest major religious text.
   C. the world's least influential major religious text.
   D. None of the above.

4. **Lao-tzu**
   A. is a historical figure whose dates of birth and death have been clearly established.
   B. is regarded by many as the author of the *Tao Te Ching*.
   C. founded Zen Buddhism.
   D. None of the above.

5. **The *Zhuangzi* is**
   A. a written set of instructions for an ancient Chinese pilgrimage.
   B. an important Taoist text.
   C. a modern essay on interfaith relations.
   D. None of the above.

6. **The *Tao Te Ching* is**

    A. longer than the *Zhuangzi.*

    B. shorter than the *Zhuangzi.*

    C. exactly the same length as the *Zhuangzi.*

    D. None of the above.

7. **The word *Tao* can be translated as**

    A. "Way."

    B. "Seafood."

    C. "Female."

    D. None of the above.

8. **A famous Taoist question asks the human being whether he or she has**

    A. accepted Rebirth from the Divine Mother.

    B. the patience to wait until the mud settles and the water is clear.

    C. a clear career goal.

    D. None of the above.

9. **True or false: Buddhism was influenced by Taoism.**

10. **True or false: Taoist principles have had little influence outside of China.**

chapter **6**

Taoism: Core Beliefs and Practices

In this chapter, you will learn about the beliefs and practices of the Taoists. When you are finished, you will be able to describe this important faith system.

CHAPTER OBJECTIVES

In this chapter, you will learn about:

- How religious belief and practice in Taoism build on the core ideas of Taoism

- The core experiences of Taoist religious practice

- The major Taoist groups

Religious beliefs and practices within Taoism emerged from the ideas of the earliest Taoist thinkers—beginning with Lao-tzu and Zhuangzi and extending into the teachings of the many later theorists. As a result, religious Taoism strongly promotes such values as simplicity, naturalness, spontaneity, the transcendence of personal desire, and of course wu-wei, "action without actions."

However, the concepts found in those early texts do not define religious Taoism as a whole. In fact, the further Taoism moves from its philosophical foundation, the more traditional Chinese cultural material it assimilates and incorporates into its scheme of worship and practice. Religious Taoism, unlike philosophical Taoism, integrates significant elements from Chinese folk culture.

The Taoist tradition now presents seemingly endless historical interactions with both Confucianism and Buddhism, as well as significant intersections with ancient Chinese folk religion within this system. In fact, all of these Eastern traditions have influenced Taoist religious belief and practice down through the centuries.

Some elements of modern Taoism related to magic, healing, longevity, and divination can be traced to prehistoric folk religions in China that later became part of the Taoist tradition. What follows is a summary of some of the key principles that have emerged from this rich historical mix.

Connection to Nature

For millennia, Chinese thought has emphasized the importance of humanity's intimate connection to nature and to the universe. This concept underlies all Taoist belief and practice and is a powerful unifying element within this faith system. It also unites Taoist belief and practice—both ancient and later—with a longstanding global tradition, both in and out of faith practice, emphasizing Nature itself as divine.

Many non-Taoist thinkers have espoused beliefs that align with religious Taoism's emphasis on the connection of human beings to the natural world they inhabit.

SPIRITUALLY SPEAKING

"Condensed into a single phrase, the injunction of Lao-tzu to mankind is, 'Follow Nature.'"

—*Lionel Giles, The Sayings of Lao Tzu*

Three Complementary Experiences

Operating within this primal reality of Taoist religious experience are three complementary experiences:

- Experience of the Tao Itself
- Experience of Chi
- Experience of the Purposeful Life

Let's look at each of these now.

The Experience of the Tao Itself

Direct experience of the Tao is the objective of religious practices such as breathing exercises, massage, martial arts, and meditation. These practices, and others, fall under the category of "internal and external alchemy," a phrase that encompasses techniques designed to bring the practitioner into closer physical and mental harmony with the Tao.

CAREFUL! *Two types of "alchemy" exist within Taoism. They should not be con-*
   fused. External alchemy is the art of mastering special breathing techniques,
   sexual practices, physical exercises, and yoga, and even attempting to produce an
   elixir for longevity and/or immortality. **Internal alchemy** *includes refined visual-*
   ization, stringent dieting, precise sexual exercises, and sexual restraint. A strict diet
   is believed to kill demons within the body and stimulates and maintains energy.
   The many different types of meditation all revolve around breathing disciplines.

Other activities, such as the recitation of the *Tao Te Ching* (thought by many to ward off bad luck and evil spirits) and the use of talismans (strips of paper bearing special images or writing) are thought to increase harmony with the Tao.

The Experience of Chi

Chi is the animating life force that promotes and sustains all growth. Direct experience of chi is central to Taoist belief and practice.

Practitioners of traditional Chinese medicine and other disciplines distinguish many different varieties of chi. Within Taoist cosmology, the two most basic forms of chi are known as Yin-qi and Yang-qi—the classic feminine and masculine energies depicted in the familiar yin-yang symbol. Note that in the traditional yin-yang symbol, each half contains an element of its opposite.

KEY TERMS DEMYSTIFIED: Chi Gung/Qigong

The traditional Taoist practice of aligning breath, movement, and mindfulness for healing, exercise, and meditation. Qigong derives from ancient principles found in Chinese medicine, martial arts, and philosophy and is understood by practitioners as a means of cultivating and balancing chi (qi).

Chi is perhaps best defined as an active principle forming part of the experience of any and every living thing. The Chinese character, which translates literally as "breath," is frequently translated as "intrinsic life energy," "life force," or "energy flow."

Chi is the foundation principle of all traditional Chinese medicine and martial arts. All these disciplines, and many others, rely on the manipulation of chi.

SPIRITUALLY SPEAKING

"The capacity to perceive the flow of qi directly—to actually see or feel it—is something that can be cultivated through training in qigong or acupuncture. Like any skill, some people are better at it than others: for some it seems to come 'naturally,' for others it's more of a challenge. Even if it's not consciously cultivated or acknowledged, most of us can tell the difference between someone who has 'great energy' and someone from whom we feel a 'bad vibe.' And most of us are able to notice, when we enter a room, whether the atmosphere seems relaxed and uplifted, or tense and heavy. To the extent that we notice such things, we are tuning into the level of qi."

—*Elizabeth Reninger, American poet*

The Experience of the Purposeful Life

To experience a purposeful life, a life that is lived both moment to moment and over the long term in harmony with the Tao, is the ideal of this faith system. This aspiration overlaps with the Zen Buddhist ideal of "beginner's mind," the Confucian principle of "mindful energy," and the mystic aspects of many other traditions.

Living in harmony with the Tao means internalizing the reality that all opposites are interrelated and that all polarities complement one another. Thus, happiness and unhappiness, love and hate, even life and death are accepted as two sides of the same coin, and neither opposite is regarded as superior to the other. A purposeful life within this practice requires accepting the proposition that clinging to opposites, fighting the natural course of things, is a recipe for disharmony.

As a religious aspiration, contemporary Taoist practitioners focus on the attainment of longevity and/or immortality, a flexible goal that is interpreted in various different ways by different subgroups. Some believe the Taoist ideal immortality to involve eternal life, while others choose to see it simply as extreme longevity; still others interpret the classical Taoist goal of immortality to mean the development of otherworldly physical powers and abilities. However it is defined, religious Taoists have pursued the goal of a long life in any number of ways, including:

- Using regulation of the breath to harness chi
- Using various meditative techniques

- Channeling sexual energies
- Pursuing other disciplines
- Cultivating moral, upright behavior that is in accordance with the Tao

Contemporary Taoist Groups

Most contemporary Taoist practitioners are located in Asia, though some groups worship outside of the continent. A breakdown of the two major schools in China follows.

Southern Taoists (active in southern China and Taiwan) claim a lineage extending back to the Cheng-i tradition, which can be traced back to the eleventh century. Taoist priests in this school perform a liturgy that is held to bring the community into harmony with the Tao. They also perform special healing ceremonies and even public exorcisms.

Northern Taoists (active elsewhere in the country) claim a different, somewhat later lineage, and de-emphasize public healings and exorcisms. Their practice is more likely to emphasize spiritual and moral development on the personal level. Less is known about this group because it was only found to have survived the religious purges of the 1960s relatively recently, and because exposure of its practices to Western observers has been less frequent.

Taoism in a Box	
Divinity	Religious Taoism as practiced in contemporary China is a polytheistic religion. The Three Pure Ones are held highest in regard. The Three Pure Ones are called Yu-ch'ing (Jade Pure), Shang-ch'ing (Upper Pure), and T'ai-ch'ing (Great Pure). They represent three aspects of the divinity inherent in all living beings. They symbolize a kind of Taoist trinity: Tao begets one; one begets two; two begets three; three begets all things.
Afterlife	One who follows Taoism tries to render death meaningless by becoming one with the Tao (Way), which leads to immortality. The body matter turns to dust and is collected into the immortal Way (Tao).
Purpose of Human Life	To live in harmony with the Tao.
Distinctive Practices and Beliefs	Gathering one's energies so that they don't become scattered, balancing the male and female energies, remaining in harmony with the cosmos, and to return to cosmic unity is to Keep the One. On certain days, food may be set out as a sacrifice to the spirits of the deceased or the gods, such as during the Qingming Festival. Burning Joss paper, or Hell Bank Notes, in order to make them available for the spirits of honored ancestors and deceased loved ones is also observed as a sacrifice.
Outsiders Often Distracted by	The historical presence of philosophical Taoism, which does not encompass all aspects of religious Taoism.

Summary

- Religious beliefs and practices within Taoism begin with Lao-tzu and Zhuangzi and extend into the teachings of the many later theorists. Religious Taoism promotes simplicity, naturalness, spontaneity, the transcendence of personal desire, and wu-wei, "action without actions."

- The further Taoism moves from its philosophical foundation, the more traditional Chinese cultural material it assimilates. Religious Taoism, unlike philosophical Taoism, integrates significant elements from Chinese folk culture. Operating within this primal reality of Taoist religious experience are three complementary experiences:

  o Experience of the Tao Itself

  o Experience of Chi

  o Experience of the Purposeful Life

QUIZ

1. Taoism holds that all human beings are connected to
   A. nature.
   B. technology.
   C. a "hungry ghost."
   D. None of the above.

2. One translation of *chi* is
   A. "literary excellence."
   B. "reincarnation."
   C. "intrinsic life energy."
   D. None of the above.

3. Most practicing Taoists are today found in
   A. Asia.
   B. Australia.
   C. North America.
   D. None of the above.

4. Religious Taoism incorporates elements of
   A. European Christianity.
   B. Nordic Atheism.
   C. Chinese folk religion.
   D. None of the above.

5. True or false: The yin-yang symbol consists of seven overlapping triangles.

6. As a religious aspiration, contemporary Taoist practitioners focus on
   A. the attainment of longevity and/or immortality.
   B. the doctrine of the physical divinity of political leaders.
   C. principles of nonviolence inherited from Buddhism.
   D. None of the above.

7. **The group known as "Southern Taoists" is active today in**
   A. southern China and Taiwan.
   B. Hong Kong only.
   C. the regions of the country located outside southern China and Taiwan.
   D. None of the above.

8. **The group known as "Northern Taoists" is active today in**
   A. southern China and Taiwan.
   B. Hong Kong only.
   C. the regions of the country located outside southern China and Taiwan.
   D. None of the above

9. **The religious practices of Northern Taoists were thought by many to have**
   A. led to the downfall of the Chinese Communists.
   B. superseded the practices of the Southern Taoists throughout China.
   C. been eradicated during the Chinese political upheavals of the 1960s.
   D. None of the above.

10. **Religious Taoism as practiced in contemporary China is**
    A. a monotheistic religion.
    B. a polytheistic religion.
    C. an agnostic religion.
    D. None of the above.

chapter 7

Shinto: History and Context

There are three different ways of approaching the history of Shinto. When you are done reading this chapter, you will be able to describe the development of this faith system.

CHAPTER OBJECTIVES

In this chapter, you will learn about:

- The prevailing historical views of Shinto
- The phases in this religion's development

Shinto is an indigenous spiritual practice of the people of Japan. The word describes a set of traditional practices that connect present-day Japan and its ancient past. The dynamic of reestablishing contact with the remote Japanese past is a distinctive element of this faith system, which has no formal dogma.

KEY TERMS DEMYSTIFIED: Shinto

This word comes from the Chinese words *Shen* ("spirits, natural forces, gods") and *Tao* ("way, path"). It thus means "The path of the spirits" or "The path of the gods." The spirits and forces in question are known as *kami* within this faith system.

One historical view of Shinto holds that it is the expression of an evolving system of religious beliefs rooted in practices that extend far back into prehistory.

Another view holds that what we today call Shinto is a relatively new religion constituted, primarily for political reasons, from a diverse and complex set of beliefs and spiritual perspectives heavily influenced by Buddhism.

SPIRITUALLY SPEAKING

"To the most holy Kami, Izanagi, who purified himself by ritual bathing in the calm sea in the morning sun—I entreat him to purify away all the impurity, disasters, sins, and faults."

—*Shinto Prayer of Purification*

A third perspective on Shinto points out that it coexists with other forms of belief in Japan and serves as a cultural and historical background for the religious experience in Japan. Proponents of this third view point out that many Japanese self-identify as both Buddhist and Shinto, arguing that Shinto is a "belief system" that actually de-emphasizes belief, at least in its modern practice, and does not exclude other (Japanese) religious perspectives.

SPIRITUALLY SPEAKING

"Shinto priests almost never . . . have stepped beyond the role of ritual practitioner to assume that of moral guide. . . . That job was largely left to . . . head of the family and community, to the Confucian scholar and in modern times to the school."

—*Ronald P. Dore, British sociologist*

Whichever of these three analyses makes the most sense—and all have merit—the emergence of the system we now call Shinto can be broken down into four main periods of time:

- The period before the arrival of Buddhism to the Japanese islands, also known as prehistory
- The period of coexistence between Shinto and Buddhism
- The reinterpretation of Shinto that took place during the nineteenth century
- Shinto after the World War II

Let's look at each of these now.

Prehistory of Shinto

In the long period that preceded the arrival of Buddhism in China in the sixth century of the Common Era, Shinto was not a formal, organized religious system. Numerous local belief traditions existed; beliefs, stories, and practices springing from these traditions would later be grouped under the umbrella term of *Shinto*.

The prehistoric communities that developed in Japan appear to have included animist faith systems that were devoted to worshiping natural spirits. These spirits are today known as kami.

> ## KEY TERMS DEMYSTIFIED: Animism
>
> The belief that naturally occurring entities—such as plants, animals, or other elements or phenomena—are worthy of worship and/or reverence, due to the spiritual essence they possess.

Rituals and stories about these spirits gave rise to a vast, complex traditional folklore that is intricately bound up with early Japanese history. It seems likely that there were other groups and other religious systems assimilated during this period—for instance, from Korean invaders who made their way into the Japanese island system in later prehistory.

Ultimately, though, all of the faith systems that evolved during this period were strongly influenced by local beliefs, customs, and experience. Instead of thinking of these as initial elements of Shinto practice, it probably makes more sense to think of them as precursor faiths with strong historic ties to Japanese culture and tradition.

Buddhist Influence

From about the sixth century CE forward, traditional animist beliefs in Japan faced major competition from Buddhism.

It was at that point that the local faith traditions that we now call Shinto began to respond to the establishment of Buddhist temples, rituals, and religious hierarchies in Japan. In addition to a "roots" movement that sought to defend and preserve ancient patterns of belief, a trend toward systematizing and combining religious practices took hold in the nation's spiritual and political lives, which were closely linked.

Soon, a blend of native religious practice, Buddhist ceremony, and Confucian ritual gave authenticity to central governing and administrative principles (such as calendar making) that informed the daily experience of Japanese life. Over time, the Japanese adapted to a system in which both Buddhist ideas and Confucian principles of etiquette coexisted—sometimes harmoniously, sometimes less so—with rituals and public duties involving kami. A philosophical movement proclaiming the emperor to be the direct descendent of Amaterasu, a minor goddess, arose during this period. It eventually led to a cult of emperor-worship that would eventually give rise to an important political doctrine in Japan. But that doctrine would come much later.

The relative influence of Buddhism and Shinto shifted many times before the middle of the nineteenth century, but the pendulum eventually swung toward a refined form of Shinto that emphasized the role of certain deities as fathers to the Japanese people. It's important to note here that all of these changes took place over long time frames and that the distinctive Japanese blend of complementary religious practices, while shifting constantly, tended to be pragmatic and to support current political institutions.

The Nineteenth Century

In 1868, the Meiji Restoration reinvented Shinto, bringing it explicitly under the control of a central administrative structure and removing supposedly foreign Buddhist influences. The emperor's role as a literal descendent of Amaterasu was emphasized by elevating that deity's status, emphasizing the emperor himself as both a major national object of worship and as the high priest of the religion. Having coexisted for more than a millennium with both Buddhist and Confucianism elements, Shinto was forcefully extracted from them and was proclaimed the state religion of Japan.

Among the notable changes at this time was the end of the practice of identifying certain kami with specific Buddhist entities from the Japanese Buddhist pantheon. A major realignment of the Japanese belief system produced a completely native pantheon.

All non-Japanese beliefs and practices were banned. Specifically, shrines were purged of Buddhist influence, and only the "purified" and centrally authorized strand of Shinto was promoted, in a form that clearly fused religious practice with Japanese nationalism. Buddhist and unofficial local influences eventually made their way back into national life, but not before Shinto had become a powerful bonding agent within Japanese society. In the form of the faith that emerged during this period, Shinto stressed the divinity of the emperor, strict devotion to certain kami, worship of ancestors, and a profound sense of duty and loyalty to both nation and family.

Post World War II

In the aftermath of Japan's defeat in World War II, Meiji-era centralized Shintoism was abruptly abandoned. It was seen as inexorably tied to the expansionist military government, particularly by the American occupational forces, which were openly hostile to the religion.

In particular, the divine and infallible nature of the emperor was seen as problematic, given both the dangerous nationalism it had previously inspired and Japan's, and thus the emperor's, defeat. If the emperor was not invincible, a core tenet of Meiji-era belief was gone, leading to deep questions about the underpinnings of the belief. Many of the more extreme expressions of Shinto belief that the military had encouraged during the war, including the infamous kamikaze bombings, had seemingly failed to defend Japan or lead it to victory.

In addition to the philosophical and theological challenges to the strict, "purified" Shinto of the Meiji Era, there were major political and military stresses that combined to depose Shinto as the official religion of Japan. The victorious American forces were eager to make sure that Japan would not return to its prewar militaristic and expansionist policies, and so dismantled much of the Imperial government. As part of the peace process, the emperor disavowed his divine status, instead basing his rule over Japan on mutual respect with his people. In addition, Japan's new constitution expressly forbids any type of state-sponsored religion or religious activity, guaranteeing freedom of religious expression instead.

Without its official mandate, and with the emperor no longer claiming godhood, the fervency and visibility of Shintoism declined in public life. There have been several revival movements aimed at revitalizing the practice of Shinto, and several new sects of the belief that have less nationalistic emphases have been established, but the overall Japanese cultural feeling has been reluctant to embrace organized Shinto as a religion. The concept of "State Shinto," what constitutes it, and to what level it is acceptable is the subject of much discussion today.

However, the practice of Shinto ceremonies and other cultural aspects of Shintoism have remained closely tied to Japanese life. Shinto as a religion, an organized system of beliefs with prescribed requirements for adherence, is not widely espoused, but certain aspects of Shinto belief, such as reverence for the natural world, ancestor worship, and the upkeep of shrines, are widely observed, even by those who do not consider themselves devout followers of Shinto. In addition, Shinto's traditional role as cornerstone of Japanese community life is still strong, and many cultural festivals, and even some Imperial ceremonies, maintain an atmosphere of Shinto mysticism and a reverence for the language and traditions of their founding.

CAREFUL! *Shinto's contemporary role in Japanese life is complex. The seeming contradiction in which adherence to strict Shinto is not widespread, and yet many Japanese homes include a traditional Shinto shrine that sees regular use, is a marker of the fluidity of religion within Japanese culture. The conception of what constitutes a "religion" is not firm or exclusive as in some other cultures.*

Confucian and Buddhist philosophy and tradition coexist with Shinto to varying degrees, often mixed and matched by any given individual based on personal needs and the needs of his or her community. Western conceptions of religious exclusivity, requiring a person to pick a single religious tradition and follow it firmly and exclusively, are not widespread in Japan.

Summary

- Shinto is the indigenous spiritual practice of the people of Japan.
- There are differing perspectives concerning the historical development of Shinto.
- Shinto emerged and developed in four phases: prehistory, Buddhist influence, the nineteenth century, and post World War II.
- The historical complexity, the connection to the Japanese islands, and the powerful communal nature of all that falls under the umbrella term *Shinto* makes this faith system distinctive.

QUIZ

1. **Shinto has**
   A. one and only one viable theory that explains its origin and development.
   B. at least three theories that explain its origin and development.
   C. no viable theories that explain its origin and development.
   D. None of the above.

2. ***Animism* means**
   A. "practice."
   B. "Asian dramatic performance."
   C. "atheism."
   D. None of the above.

3. **Shinto is the indigenous spiritual practice of**
   A. Japan.
   B. China.
   C. North America.
   D. None of the above.

4. **Buddhism**
   A. eradicated Shinto.
   B. coexists with Shinto.
   C. was eradicated by Shinto.
   D. None of the above.

5. **Shinto, Confucian, and Buddhist philosophy and tradition**
   A. are never practiced in contemporary Japan.
   B. have now been consolidated into a single official Japanese religion.
   C. were not practiced in Japan prior to World War II.
   D. None of the above.

6. **In 1868, the Meiji Restoration**
   A. reinvented Shinto, bringing it explicitly under the control of a central administrative structure.
   B. banned Shinto.
   C. created Shinto missionary centers in England.
   D. None of the above.

7. **The officials of the Meiji Restoration**

    A. were generally hostile to perceived non-Japanese influences on Shinto.

    B. were generally open to perceived non-Japanese influences on Shinto.

    C. were indifferent to perceived non-Japanese influences on Shinto.

8. **True or false: Confucian and Buddhist traditions now coexist with Shinto.**

9. **After World War II, the formal practice of Shinto de-emphasized beliefs and practices related to**

    A. the divine nature of the emperor and his family.

    B. nature.

    C. requests for blessings.

    D. None of the above.

10. **In the years since the end of World War II, Shinto has become**

    A. more fervent and more visible in Japanese public life.

    B. less fervent and less visible in Japanese public life.

    C. indistinguishable from Chinese Taoism.

    D. None of the above.

chapter 8

Shinto: Core Beliefs and Practices

It's time to learn about the beliefs and practices associated with Shinto.

CHAPTER OBJECTIVES

In this chapter, you will learn about:

- What kami are
- The main purposes of Shinto rituals
- How Shinto practitioners express their faith

Important aspects of Shinto include its beliefs regarding kami, the place of rituals and shrines, Shinto's festivals, and its texts.

The Kami

Understanding the beliefs of Shinto begins with understanding the entities known as *kami*. Historically, kami can be elements of the landscape, forces of nature, or even the emperor himself. (This political aspect of Shinto has been de-emphasized since World War II.) Kami take countless forms—tradition holds that there are eight million of them—but all are expressions of nature that cause awe, and all are regarded as capable of shifting both natural occurrences and the stream of human events.

> ## KEY TERMS DEMYSTIFIED: **Kami**
>
> Phenomena or spirits regarded as objects of worship within the religion of Shinto. The term encompasses a wide variety of elements, including natural phenomena, spirits, ancestors, and other figures, all of which are regarded as being part of nature rather than separate from nature.

CAREFUL! *Drawing clear lines between the important figures of Shinto and those of other faith systems can be a difficult business. Shinto is an inclusive faith system that has successfully adopted countless objects of worship from a wide variety of traditions. The kami, for instance, have included both Buddhas and the God of the Hebrew scriptures.*

Shinto Rituals

Shinto has many rituals by which practitioners express their faith. The purpose of most of them is to ward off evil spirits or seek assistance. These goals are accomplished through purification, prayers, and making offerings. Some rituals also focus on the cleansing of sins; Shintoism teaches that people should want their misdeeds cleansed both for the sake of their own personal peace and harmony and in order to be pure enough to approach the kami.

Purification rituals, known as harae, are an essential part of Shinto, initiating all formal ceremonies. Water and salt are typically important parts of these rituals. Purification is held to follow the example of the legendary Izangi No-mikoto, who ventured into the Land of the Dead to visit his wife, and then washed himself free of the pollution of that journey.

Other rituals involve blessings. Places where followers of Shintoism intend to spend a lot of time, such as a new home, are often blessed by a priest during the groundbreaking ceremony. This ancient practice has been successfully and seamlessly adapted into the modern world of Japan. (For example, Japanese cars are likely to be blessed during assembly.)

KEY TERMS DEMYSTIFIED: Misogi, Kagura, and Ema

Misogi is a purification ritual using water. It is typically performed by Shinto worshippers before entering a shrine. **Kagura** is an ancient Shinto ritual dance. Tradition holds that it once involved actual possession by the kami invoked during the dance; modern expression pays homage to these shamanic elements but does not attempt to produce spirit possession. **Ema** are small wooden plaques Shinto believers use to record written supplications. They are then left at a shrine in the hope that kami will receive them.

Ema are small wooden plaques believers use to record written supplications at Shinto shrines.

Credit: Irene Alastruey/Punchstock

Shinto Shrines

Followers of Shinto honor kami and seek good fortune at shrines of many kinds. There are more than 100,000 Shinto shrines in Japan. Each has the purpose of serving as a home for one or more kami.

A gatelike structure known as a torii has become a familiar visual symbol for Shinto itself. The shrine's most important structure, however, is the honden, or sanctuary, which provides a safe place for sacred objects of various kinds and serves as a dwelling place for kami; this space is usually reserved for priests and priestesses. The honden may be absent if the shrine stands on or in the object being worshipped (a mountain, for instance), or if objects believed to attract the spirits known as yorishori, held to provide contact with kami, are near.

The torii, which has become emblematic of Shinto.

Credit: © image 100/Corbix

KEY TERMS DEMYSTIFIED: **Shinto Priesthood**

Today, the Shinto priesthood is open to both men and women. Priests may marry and raise a family.

There is no obligatory weekly religious service that Shinto practitioners must attend, though some make a habit of frequenting ceremonies on the first and fifteenth of the month. Many people simply visit shrines when it is convenient for them to do so.

Shinto Festivals

Shinto has a number of major festivals every year, including the Spring Festival, the Autumn or Harvest Festival, the Annual Festival, and the Divine Procession.

SPIRITUALLY SPEAKING

"Large (Shinto) festivals . . . are held at the turning points between seasons. All of the seasonal changes are related to rice farming, since rice cultivation is one of the most important traditional livelihoods for the Japanese. In the spring festival, people pray for a rich and bountiful harvest. In the autumn, villagers thank the deity for providing the season's crops. In the hot humid season of summer festivals, community prayers go towards driving away disasters and misfortune. At the winter festivals, they pray for the revival of life and rich harvest for the coming spring. There are significant offerings for the deity at these festivals such as food offerings and traditional court music and dance. People offer premium rice, sake, water, salt, seasonal vegetables, seasonal fruits, meats and fish for the deity. After the offering, people share these foods in order to gain spiritual strength from the deity."

—*Jinja Honcho, Association of Shinto Shrines*

Shinto Texts

The Shinto religion follows a number of important texts. These include:

- The *Kojiki* ("Record of Ancient Matters"). This culturally vital collection of Japanese myths covers the origin of the four main islands of Japan and of the kami. It is believed to have been commissioned by the Empress Gemmei in the early eighth century CE.
- The *Rikkokushi* ("Six National Histories") are a collection of chronicles describing both the history and mythology of Japan, composed during the eighth and ninth centuries CE by the order of the Japanese emperors of that period. The sources for the accounts were official records of the time. The collection comprises the *Nihongi*, which covers the mythical period through to the year 697 CE; the *Shokki*, which covers the period from 697 to 791; the *Nihon Koki*, which covers the period from 792 through 833; the *Shoku Nihon Koki*, which covers the period from 833 through 850; the *Nihon Montoku Tenno Jitsoroku*, which covers the period from 850 through 858; and the *Nihon Sandai Jistoruku*, which covers the period from 858 through 887.
- The *Shoku Nihongi* and its *Nihon Shoki* ("Continuing Chronicles of Japan").
- The *Jinno Shotoki*, a much later study of Shinto and Japanese politics and history that emphatically proclaimed the divinity of the Japanese home islands.

Shinto in a Box	
Divinity	Shinto is focused on the kami, and worships the essence or soul of anything natural that inspires awe. The most important kami include Amaterasu Omikami, the Sun Goddess and ancestress of the Imperial family, and the kamikaze or "divine wind."
Afterlife	People who die become kami; those who die in peace, surrounded by family, become revered ancestors. Those who don't may become "hungry ghosts" and cause difficulties for the living.
Purpose of Human Life	Shinto followers are supposed to live in harmony and peaceful coexistence with each other and with nature.
Distinctive Practices and Beliefs	Shinto is not an exclusive religion. It accepts the principle that it can be complemented by an additional religion. Water is important in purification, as are recitation of prayers and the use of amulets and protective objects.
Outsiders Often Distracted by	Animé (Japanese cartoons) and manga (Japanese comic books). Classic Shinto narratives inspire many of these stories, but the commercially driven, modern graphic art retellings are not to be mistaken for the real thing.

Summary

- Kami are phenomena or spirits regarded as objects of worship within the religion of Shinto. The term encompasses natural phenomena, spirits, ancestors, and other figures, all of which are regarded as being part of nature.

- Shinto is an inclusive faith system that has successfully adopted countless objects of worship from a wide variety of traditions.

- Shinto has many rituals to ward off evil spirits or seek assistance through purification, prayers, and making offerings. Some rituals also focus on the cleansing of sins for the sake of personal peace and harmony, and in order to be pure enough to approach the kami.

QUIZ

1. **Kami are**
   A. phenomena or spirits regarded as objects of worship within the religion of Shinto.
   B. early Japanese weavers.
   C. modern folk songs celebrating the intersection of nature and technology.
   D. None of the above.

2. **Shinto is**
   A. an exclusive religion that has never adapted figures of worship from other sources.
   B. an inclusive religion that has adapted figures of worship from other sources.
   C. based on the teachings of the first Shinto priest.
   D. None of the above.

3. **A major objective of Shinto ritual is**
   A. to summon evil spirits.
   B. to ward off evil spirits.
   C. to create a level of concentrated meditation.
   D. None of the above.

4. **The Shinto priesthood is now**
   A. open only to men.
   B. open only to women.
   C. open to both men and women.
   D. no longer active.

5. **The *Kojiki* is**
   A. a purification rite.
   B. an important Shinto text.
   C. a major Japanese auto plant.
   D. None of the above.

6. **The Divine Procession is**
   A. an annual television broadcast.
   B. an important Shinto festival.
   C. a kami.
   D. None of the above.

7. **Purification is important in Shinto because**

    A. all human beings are regarded as inherently evil.

    B. only priests may be purified.

    C. those who are ritually impure cannot approach the kami.

    D. None of the above.

8. **The word *Rikkokushi* translates as**

    A. "Six National Histories."

    B. "worship of the emperor."

    C. "creativity."

    D. None of the above.

9. **True or false: There is no obligatory weekly Shinto worship service.**

10. **True or false: The God of the Hebrew scriptures has been incorporated as an object of worship within Shinto.**

PART ONE TEST

This test assesses your mastery of ancient religious traditions and will help you prepare for the Final Exam at the end of the book. You will identify which, if any, of the four ancient religious traditions you've just studied should be reviewed more closely before you tackle that test.

Schedule a half hour to an hour of uninterrupted time to see just how well you have mastered the content presented in Chapters 1 through 8. This preliminary test will tell you where you are strongest—and where you still need to review content relating to Hinduism, Buddhism, Taoism, and Shinto.

1. **Bhakti is the active, loving _____ activity of a worshipper toward the Divine.**
   A. devotional
   B. craft-focused
   C. physics
   D. vacation

2. **The *Bhagavad Gita* presents the Lord Krishna as a divine teacher, in discussion with Prince**
   A. Avalokitesvara.
   B. Gautama.
   C. Charles.
   D. Arjuna.

3. **The Hindu god of creation is**
   A. Brahma.
   B. Brahman.
   C. Brahmin.
   D. None of the above.

4. **True or false: Dharma is seen as having no beginning and no end.**

5. **The Indus River Valley Civilization thrived from about**
   A. 3300 BCE to 1500 BCE.
   B. 1000 CE to 1500 CE.
   C. 1500 CE to 1948 CE.
   D. None of the above.

6. **Karma is a central principle of**

    A. Buddhism and Hinduism.

    B. Hinduism and Christianity.

    C. Christianity and Taoism.

    D. Shinto and Christianity.

7. **Pantheism is the worship of**

    A. many gods.

    B. one God.

    C. the Universe (or Nature) in all its manifestations, or the belief that everything is divine.

    D. None of the above.

8. **Reincarnation is a central principle of**

    A. Buddhism and Hinduism.

    B. Hinduism and Christianity.

    C. Christianity and Taoism.

    D. Shinto and Christianity.

9. **Shaktism is a great devotional school within Hinduism whose object of veneration is _____ , the ancient goddess figure.**

    A. Shakti

    B. Devi

    C. Parvati

    D. All of the above.

10. **The Vedas are**

    A. the oldest surviving examples of Indian literature.

    B. the oldest scriptures of Hinduism.

    C. broken down into four groups: the Rigveda, the Yajurveda, the Samaveda, and the Atharaveda.

    D. All of the above.

11. **Sanskrit is**

    A. the ancient language of both Hindu and Buddhist texts.

    B. the ancient language of only Buddhist texts.

    C. the modern language spoken by North American Buddhists.

    D. None of the above.

12. **The word *Buddha* means**

   A. "Precise Image."

   B. "Rest and Relaxation."

   C. "Awakened One" or "Enlightened One."

   D. None of the above.

13. **An ascetic is someone who**

   A. indulges all the senses for religious reasons.

   B. abstains from all indulgence.

   C. makes sarcastic remarks.

   D. None of the above.

14. **Nirvana was described in this book as**

   A. a joke.

   B. a beam of light that never lands anywhere.

   C. an interfaith conference.

   D. All of the above.

15. **The Theravada school is**

   A. the dominant mode of religious expression in Sri Lanka and much of Southeast Asia.

   D. the dominant form of Buddhism in northern Asia.

   C. the dominant form of Buddhism in Tibet.

   D. All of the above.

16. **The Mahayana school is**

   A. the dominant mode of religious expression in Sri Lanka and much of Southeast Asia.

   B. the dominant form of Buddhism in northern Asia.

   C. the dominant form of Buddhism in Tibet.

   D. All of the above.

17. **The Vajrayana school is**

   A. the dominant mode of religious expression in Sri Lanka and much of Southeast Asia.

   B. the dominant form of Buddhism in northern Asia.

   C. the dominant form of Buddhism in Tibet.

   D. All of the above.

18. **One translation from Sanskrit to English defines** *samsara* **as**
    A. "forgotten wave."
    B. "endless sleep."
    C. "continuous movement."
    D. "cotton garment."

19. **The Four Noble Truths examine the source and remedy for human**
    A. evolution.
    B. enlightenment.
    C. suffering.
    D. All of the above.

20. **The Eightfold Path is the subject of Buddhism's**
    A. First Noble Truth.
    B. Second Noble Truth.
    C. Third Noble Truth.
    D. Fourth Noble Truth.

21. **The Tao can be defined as the fundamental principle underlying the _____, "the way things are."**
    A. university
    B. video
    C. universe
    D. All of the above.

22. *Wu-wei* **is a central concept in Taoism that literally means**
    A. "nonaction or nondoing."
    B. "action or doing."
    C. "presentableness."
    D. "None of the above."

23. **Confucianism is an important ethical and philosophical system based on the principles of the ancient Chinese philosopher**
    A. Master King.
    B. Master Kong.
    C. Lao-tzu.
    D. None of the above.

24. **The title of the *Tao Te Ching* can be translated**

    A. "The Great Book of the Way and the Power."

    B. "The Small Book of the Way and the Power."

    C. "The Lost Book of the Way and the Power."

    D. None of the above.

25. **The *Zhuangzi*'s title is also the name of**

    A. the period in which the book was composed.

    B. the author of the text.

    C. the monarch to whom the book is dedicated.

    D. None of the above.

26. **External alchemy is the art of mastering special breathing techniques, sexual practices, physical exercises, yoga, and even attempting to produce an elixir for**

    A. longevity and/or immortality.

    B. clear skin.

    C. better language skills.

    D. None of the above.

27. **Internal alchemy includes refined visualization, stringent dieting, and precise _____ exercises.**

    A. sexual

    B. vocal

    C. memory

    D. None of the above.

28. **Chi gung, also called qigong, is the traditional Taoist practice of aligning breath, movement, and mindfulness for healing, exercise, and**

    A. government pensions.

    B. political satire.

    C. meditation.

    D. None of the above.

29. **Shinto is an indigenous spiritual practice of the people of**

    A. China.

    B. Korea.

    C. Japan.

    D. None of the above.

30. The word *Shinto* comes from the Chinese words *Shen* ("spirits, natural forces, gods") and _____ ("way, path").

    A. *Tao*
    B. *Te*
    C. *Teng*
    D. None of the above.

31. *Shinto* **therefore means**

    A. "the path of the spirits" or "the path of the gods."
    B. "the heavenly burden."
    C. "the lack of impediment."
    D. None of the above.

32. **Spirits in Shinto are known as**

    A. kami.
    B. torii.
    C. nisei.
    D. None of the above.

33. **Animism is the belief that naturally occurring entities—such as plants, animals, or other elements or phenomena—are worthy of _____ due to the spiritual essence they possess.**

    A. worship and/or reverence
    B. disregard
    C. contempt
    D. None of the above.

34. **True or false: Misogi is a purification ritual using water. It is typically performed by Shinto worshippers before entering a shrine.**

35. **Kagura is an ancient Shinto ritual dance that, tradition holds, once involved actual**

    A. possession by spirits.
    B. human sacrifice.
    C. financial transactions between the dancer and the audience.
    D. None of the above.

36. Ema are small wooden plaques Shinto believers use to

 A. improve hand/eye coordination.

 B. encourage imaginative play.

 C. record written supplications for gods/spirits.

 D. None of the above.

Part Two

The One-God Principle: Judaism, Christianity, and Islam

The impulse to proclaim and support a monotheistic (single-God) faith has informed many of humanity's religious movements. This impulse has led to differing perspectives, to countless conflicts, and to countless great works through the centuries.

The three great monotheistic traditions you will learn about in this part of the book—Judaism, Christianity, and Islam—share a great deal and are divided on a great deal. As you read, consider asking questions like, Where are the similarities? Where are the differences? And what are the real-world possibilities for tolerance, dialogue, and coexistence?

Judaism: History and Context

When you complete this chapter, you will be able to explain key points in the history of Judaism.

CHAPTER OBJECTIVES

In this chapter, you will learn about:

- Who Abraham was

- The covenant

- Judaism's conception of monotheism

- The Tanakh

- Persecution against Jews in ancient and modern times

Judaism, whose most familiar symbol is the six-pointed Star of David, is the first recorded monotheistic religion. Its development, which spans three millennia, is far older than the symbol, and its impact has been, and remains, immense.

The familiar six-pointed Star of David.
Credit: Photodisc

KEY TERMS DEMYSTIFIED: **Monotheism**

The worship of a single God. Major faith systems whose adherents describe themselves as monotheistic include Judaism, Christianity, and Islam. Judaism's monotheism is strict, regarding God as singular, nonphysical, all-knowing, all-powerful, and eternal. Statements in the Hebrew Scriptures referring to aspects of the Divine as being similar to aspects of human beings are considered to be metaphorical or semantic vehicles, necessary because without them it would be impossible to communicate about God. Representations of God as human, as trinitarian in nature, or as taking the form of multiple deities are seen as heretical for Jews.

Given its enormous influence on the history of religion, on the ancient world, and on pre-modern and modern times, its comparatively small size may come as a surprise. Throughout its long history, Judaism has often been seen as a minority faith. When we consult the modern population tables for numerical estimates of its followers, we learn that there are today only about 16 million Jews on earth, out of a total world population of seven billion.

The word *only* is used here not in disparagement, but in profound respect. Why? Because when we consider the immense religious, cultural, and social contributions that arise directly or indirectly from the Jewish faith tradition, and when we realize that these contributions confound any brief summary or description, the modest dimensions of the global body of self-describing Jews, both now and in ancient times, is nothing short of astonishing.

There are more practicing Sikhs and Shintos than practicing Jews, and far more atheists and agnostics. Yet somehow the tradition of those Jews who live and practice today, like those who lived and practiced in centuries past, seems tied to something in human religious history that overrides the numbers and makes superficial comparisons with larger groups seem both misleading and irrelevant.

That "something" is what we offer in this chapter as the key to understanding the history of Judaism: the monotheistic tradition.

Abraham and Monotheism

Judaism's history matters to human history because of its clear embrace of monotheism. With this world-changing principle, the history of the Hebrew religious tradition we now call Judaism begins.

The starting point is thought to be located somewhere around the nineteenth century BCE. The single idea uniting believers is a rigorous monotheism rooted in a divine covenant with the Hebrew people. And the individual who shared that idea was the prophet Abraham, the great first patriarch of the monotheistic tradition.

SPIRITUALLY SPEAKING

"Abraham is an extraordinary figure, in that almost alone of the Biblical characters he unites, or has the potential to unite, the three great monotheistic religions: Christianity, Judaism, and Islam. He's there in all of them—he's important in all of them. In the Christian mass, Abraham is mentioned specifically; when Muslims pray five times a day, they mention Abraham in that connection; and when Jews look back in the Torah, particularly to the covenant they made with Yahweh that made them Yahweh's chosen people, that was done through Abraham. He's the father of all faiths."

—*Peter Stanford, English writer and journalist*

The Torah
Credit: © Comstock Select/Corbis

Technically, of course, the history of Judaism begins with God's creation of the universe, which is recounted in the first chapter of Genesis in the sacred book known as the Tanakh. Historically, however, the story of Judaism begins in the part of the world we know now as the Middle East close to 3,000 years ago, with the emergence of a single community of monotheists known as Hebrews. And for the Hebrews, the story of faith began with the story of Abraham.

KEY TERMS DEMYSTIFIED: Tanakh

The distinctive Hebrew term for Judaism's core religious scriptures, beginning with the book of Genesis (Hebrew: *Bere'sit*, for "in the beginning [He] created") and ending with the book of Chronicles (Hebrew: *Dibh're Hayyamim*, for "the matters [of] the days"). It is also known as the Hebrew Bible. This collection of scriptures is often referred to by outsiders, and particularly by Christians, as the Old Testament, but that term is best avoided in interfaith discussions, if only because it presumes the existence of a newer, presumably more authoritative testament. This idea is rejected by mainstream Judaism. The Tanakh comprises the **Torah** (the first five books), the **Nevi'in** (books about various prophets), and the **Ketuvim** (a catchall term literally meaning "writings" applied to a later group of scriptures not included in the first two categories). The word **TaNaKh** is thus an ancient acronym of the Hebrew names of these three collections.

From Abram to Abraham

The first we hear of Abraham is in the eleventh chapter of the book of Genesis. When we meet him there, he is called Abram, a shepherd living in what we would today call Iraq, during a time when polytheism, the worship of many gods, is the dominant religious tradition.

What happens? Abram rejects the polytheists and accepts the one true God; God then instructs Abram to leave his native land and begin a new life in the land of Canaan, a region corresponding roughly to modern-day Israel, the Palestinian territories, Lebanon, and west Jordan.

According to Genesis, God makes three promises to Abram for his obedience: closeness to God, many descendants, and a new land. Yet at least one of these promises seems impossible for God to fulfill: the promise of many descendants. Abram and his wife are, after all, elderly and without children! Nevertheless, Abram places complete trust in, and enters into a covenant with, the one God. Miraculously, Abram does become a father—first with his handmaiden Hagar and eventually with his wife, Sarah. He also receives a new name: Abraham, the "father of many nations."

Abram undergoes many trials. His greatest test, the book of Genesis tells us, comes when he is commanded by God to sacrifice his beloved son Isaac.

Just as Abraham embarked upon this task, however, he found himself prevented from killing his son by an angel, and awarded a ram with which to conduct the sacrifice. His unswerving obedience to God having been confirmed, Abraham received a repetition of the Divine promise of numerous descendants and abundant prosperity. (A side note: In the Islamic tradition, recounted in the Qur'an, it is not Isaac but the older son, Ishmael, who is submitted for sacrifice.)

CAREFUL! *What was the name of the son whom Abraham nearly sacrificed? Jews agree it was Isaac, but Muslims follow a different narrative, identifying Ismail (Ishmael) as the son in this incident.*

The Covenant

Abraham's covenant, or binding agreement, with God, undertaken on behalf of himself and his descendants, marks the culmination of a series of covenants with humankind. (In the earlier chapters of Genesis, Adam and Noah take part in divine covenants as well.)

Abraham, his son Isaac, and Isaac's son Jacob are referred to as the Patriarchs of this faith. They are generally regarded as the founders of the religion we know today as Judaism. In a formal sense, however, it is not quite accurate to call them Jews, since the words *Jew* and *Judaism* were not applied to the nation of believers they founded until centuries after they had lived their lives.

Even so, Abraham, Isaac, and Jacob are commonly understood as, and generally considered by most Jews to be, members of the faith system historically followed by Jews. A minority view does not consider these men the founders of the faith but accords that honor to the establishment of a set of laws under the prophet Moses. Because of the strong connection of Moses to the Ten Commandments, we will examine his role in our next chapter, on belief. For our purposes now, however, Abraham and his son and grandson mark the most important starting point because the Jewish tradition of monotheism begins with Abraham's decision to trust in and obey the one Supreme Being.

The faith continues its development with the near-sacrifice of Abraham's son Isaac, and then with the birth of Isaac's son Jacob, who comes to be known by the name Israel. The monotheistic tradition is carried on by Jacob's twelve sons, who founded the twelve tribes of Israel.

SPIRITUALLY SPEAKING

"Biblical tradition holds that the 12 tribes of Israel are descended from the sons and grandsons of Jacob (Genesis 29–30; 35:16–18; 48:5–6). The tribes are collectively called Israel because of their origin in the patriarch Jacob-Israel."

—Encyclopedia Judaica

It is in Abraham's story that we see the dawn of the belief that there is one God who creates a special covenant with a specific nation; it is in his story that we begin to see the effort of the members of that nation to obey God and live lives of righteousness in gratitude for God's many favors; and it is in his story that we begin to address, through his descendants, some of the most fundamental questions of human existence: What is the purpose of human life? Why are we born? What is death? How do we live a good life?

SPIRITUALLY SPEAKING

"I will make you a great nation
And I will bless you;
I will make your name great,
And you will be a blessing
I will bless those who bless you,
And whoever curses you I will curse;
And all the peoples of the earth
Will be blessed through you."

—*God speaks to Abraham, Genesis 12:1–3*

Abraham's great journey marks not just the starting point of Jewish monotheism but also the starting point of an enduring tradition of human spiritual effort—the effort to earn a personal reconciliation with the one God. The long struggle of the Jewish people to secure both righteousness and justice extends that journey to the present day.

"According to the Bible, Abraham is humanity's last chance to establish a relationship with God. At the beginning of the Bible in the creation narratives, Adam and Eve set in train a pattern of disobedience to God's commands which takes root. Even after the Great Flood, in which only Noah was saved, humanity once again comes perilously close to alienating themselves from their creator God. They build the tower of Babel (Genesis 11), a tower that seems like it will almost break through to the heavens, and God again intervenes and scatters the people across the earth."

—*British Broadcasting Corporation, from* On Judaism

Remembrance and Trial in Judaism: A Simplified Historical Timeline

A concise summary of the complex political and social legacy of the Jewish people, from a Jewish perspective, follows. It is a history that includes both triumph and persecution.

Bronze Age–63 BCE   God chooses Abraham as forefather and first role model for a monotheistic Hebrew nation that benefits from, and must live up to, a special divine covenant. The Hebrews are guided through many trials by God; Moses leads the Hebrews out of bondage in Egypt and delivers to them a code of laws by which to live. A sequence of important kings—including Saul, David, and Solomon—bring Israel to prominence. Solomon builds the First Temple, which holds the Ark of the Covenant.

At about the same time, the Assyrian kingdom gains strength; in the centuries following the completion of the First Temple, Israel is split into two kingdoms, the Assyrians conquer northern Israel, and the Jewish people divide into smaller groups. Prophets warn the people to repent. About 422 BCE, the Babylonians conquer Israel and the First Temple is destroyed. Many Jews are exiled to Babylon, beginning the *diaspora*, or scattering of Jews beyond Israel to foreign lands. Decades later, some Jews return and begin to rebuild; in 352 CE, work begins on the construction of the Second Temple.

A series of empires dominate the Jewish people; one, the Seleucid Empire of the Greeks, meets with organized resistance in the form of the Maccabean Revolt. The Romans follow the Greeks as the dominant political and military authority in the region and invade Israel in 63 BCE.

63 BCE–1096 CE

A long period of Roman dominance is marked by political figures like Herod the Great and by organized Jewish revolt against the Roman Empire in 67 CE. The Romans crush the rebellion, and the Second Temple is destroyed in 70 CE.

The Roman Emperor Constantine embraces Christianity in 312 CE. Roman authorities ban the building of synagogues in 439 CE. The Western Roman Empire falls around 476 CE, and the Eastern Roman Empire, or Byzantine Empire, rises to a position of dominance in world affairs. Muslim armies invade and rule Jerusalem beginning in 638 CE and continue to rule in the region for more than four centuries. Muslims construct the Dome of the Rock over the spot held by Jews to be the place of Abraham's intended sacrifice of Isaac. A Golden Age of Jews in Spain begins under Muslim rule there, emphasizing science, Hebrew literature, and religious studies.

1096 CE–1600 CE

The European Crusaders begin their attempt to capture the Holy Land in 1096; European Jews are frequently attacked by the Christian armies on their way to Jerusalem. Jews and Muslims were slaughtered wholesale in Jerusalem following Christian victories there. The Crusaders were eventually forced out of the region, but the period was marked by extensive bias against and persecution of Jews in Europe, including the exile of all Jews from southern Spain following the invasion of the Berbers. Massacres and false accusations (often involving the supposed ritual murder of children) were common, as was political pressure to segregate Jews into ghettos. Jews were expelled from England in 1290, expelled from all of Spain in 1492, and targeted for abuse from the pulpit by countless Christian religious leaders. The various Jewish communities continued to thrive, and even to make great scholarly and literary contributions, despite such oppression.

1600 CE–1933 CE

Although Jews returned to England and began to establish themselves in the Americas at the beginning of this period, the catalogue of horror and persecution continued. The long history of prejudice and violence against Jews continued in many places, notably central Europe and Russia.

Political Zionism—the movement for a homeland for the Jewish people—began in Europe in the mid-nineteenth century, and took as its inspiration the centuries-old religious instinct to return to the land of Israel. At the same time, some countries, including England, eased or abolished political and social policies that discriminated against the Jewish people. Other parts of the world, however, only intensified the oppression against Jews. In Russia, a series of bloody persecutions and dislocations known as *pogroms* played out in the nineteenth century. And in Germany, the fanatically anti-Semitic National Socialist Party came to power in 1933 under the leadership of Adolf Hitler, whose ideology and ambitions helped to spark the Second World War.

1933 CE–Present

Hitler's lethal, systemic anti-Semitism in Germany brought a new level of legal and social persecution of the Jews that culminated in the Holocaust, a massive extermination campaign that eventually spread across much of Europe and killed six million people, one million of them children. Global disgust at Hitler's campaign against the Jews led to increased support for a Jewish state in British-controlled Palestine, where a modern state of Israel was established in 1948.

Summary

- Judaism is the first recorded monotheistic faith system.

- Judaism's historical and social influence is immense.

- Judaism's history matters to human history because of its clear embrace of monotheism. With this world-changing principle, the history of the Hebrew religious tradition we now call Judaism begins.

- This faith's starting point is thought to be located somewhere around the nineteenth century CE.

- The Patriarch Abraham's covenant, or binding agreement, with God, undertaken on behalf of himself and his descendants, is believed by Jews to mark the culmination of a series of covenants with humankind.

- The complex political and social legacy of the Jewish people includes both triumph and persecution.

QUIZ

1. **Monotheism is**

   A. the belief in one God.

   B. the belief in multiple Gods.

   C. the belief in God incarnated in a human being.

   D. None of the above.

2. **Today, there are about**

   A. 1.6 million Jews.

   B. 16 million Jews.

   C. 116 million Jews.

   D. None of the above.

3. **Jewish scriptural tradition holds that the twelve tribes of Israel are descended from**

   A. Ishmael.

   B. Barabbas.

   C. Jacob and his sons.

   D. None of the above.

4. **A covenant is**

   A. a binding agreement.

   B. a divorce.

   C. a birth certificate.

   D. None of the above.

5. **Abraham's story is found in**

   A. the Tanakh.

   B. the New Testament.

   C. the *Bhagavad Gita*.

   D. None of the above.

6. **An organized Jewish revolt against the Roman Empire took place in**

   A. 57 CE.

   B. 67 CE.

   C. 77 CE.

   D. 87 CE.

7. **The Romans crushed the Jewish rebellion and destroyed the Second Temple in**

    A. 60 CE.

    B. 70 CE.

    C. 80 CE.

    D. 90 CE.

8. **A Jewish Golden Age unfolded in Spain under the rule of the**

    A. Romans.

    B. Muslims.

    C. Greeks.

    D. None of the above.

9. **True or false: Hitler's campaign against the Jews in Germany was the only recorded example of the persecution of the Jews in Europe's history.**

10. **Abraham's name was originally**

    A. Abram.

    B. Ram.

    C. Bram.

    D. None of the above.

chapter **10**

Judaism: Core Beliefs and Practices

When you complete this chapter, you will be able to describe some of the most important beliefs and practices within Judaism. You will also get a sense of the geographic placement of Judaism's followers, the different denominations within the faith, the religion's size in comparison with other traditions, and the main forms of worship observed by Jews.

CHAPTER OBJECTIVES

In this chapter, you will learn about:

- Core Jewish beliefs
- Core Jewish worship practices
- Major Jewish denominations

Answering the seemingly simple question, "What do Jewish people believe?" is a good deal more difficult than it might at first appear. As ancient and as influential as it is, Judaism has no simple set of required beliefs, no generally accepted list of core tenets on which every Jew agrees—beyond the basic proposition of monotheism and the embrace of certain scriptures. Beyond this, some guiding principles are broadly accepted, but even those are subject to vigorous debate. There is no standard profession of faith that "creates" Jewishness.

This state of affairs may come as a surprise to someone who is attempting to gain an initial understanding of Judaism. The picture becomes a little clearer to outsiders, though, once we move away from the concept of religious *orthodoxy*—meaning "required beliefs"—and toward the concept of religious *orthopraxy*—"required behavior." Action counts for much more than dogmatic belief within Judaism.

> ## KEY TERMS DEMYSTIFIED: Orthopraxy
>
> Correctness in action or practice. Orthopraxy emphasizes ethical conduct in a religious and social context. It stands in contrast to orthodoxy, which emphasizes correct belief. Orthopraxy could also be described as the position that holds correct behavior to be at least as important as the acceptance of the correct religious belief system.

The emphasis on action makes sense, because this faith system is all about what happens in relationships: relationships between humanity and God, between the land of Israel and the rest of humankind, and between individual human beings. Specifically, it is about the choices within those relationships. A famous rabbi, Hillel, was once challenged to give an accurate summation of Judaism while standing on one foot. He lifted his foot and said, "Do not do to your neighbor what you yourself hate. That is the Torah, and all the rest is commentary. Now go study."

The rabbi had brilliantly underlined Judaism's emphasis on *doing*. Although it would be a mistake to say that formal belief plays no role in Judaism, it would be an even bigger mistake to overlook its strong emphasis on ethical conduct in the real world. (Hillel's response was also a reformulation of the Golden Rule, an ethical principle appearing in many religious traditions.)

KEY TERMS DEMYSTIFIED: **The Golden Rule**

This appears prominently in the Jewish religious tradition, as well as in that of Christianity, Islam, Buddhism, Hinduism, and other influential faith systems. In its various expressions, the Golden Rule maintains that what one would wish to experience personally should guide the behavior one employs in interactions with others. (The phrase Golden Rule only dates to the 1700s; the underlying concept can be traced back to at least the ancient Greeks.)

An early expression of the Golden Rule appears in the Hebrew Scriptures (Leviticus 19:18): "You shall not take vengeance or bear a grudge against your kinsfolk. Love your neighbor as yourself: I am the LORD."

Personal Belief, Community, and Desire

As we have seen, Judaism is a monotheistic faith, meaning that Jews believe there is only One God. Yet how individual Jews understand God varies. Some connect with God through formal prayer, others see the divine in the majesty of the natural world, others may not think about God on a daily basis. Each individual's relationship with God is unique and personal.

Jewish belief is connected in complex ways to Jewish identity. One answer to the common question, "Who is a Jew?" is "A member of the people and cultural community whose traditional religion is Judaism, and who trace their origins through the ancient Hebrew people of Israel to Abraham." Judaism holds that Jews are distinctively connected to each other. Regardless of where they live in the world, all Jews are part of a global Jewish community.

Judaism teaches, however, that everyone, Jewish and non-Jewish, was created "b'tzelem Elohim," which is Hebrew for "in the image of God." Thus everyone is equally important and has unlimited potential to be of benefit to the world. People have the free will to make choices in their lives, and each of us is responsible for the consequences of those choices.

13 Principles

The closest that anyone has ever come to creating a widely accepted list of Jewish beliefs is Rambam's 13 principles of faith. Rambam, the preeminent medieval

Jewish philosopher also known as Maimonides, believed these principles to be the minimum requirements of Jewish belief:

1. God exists.
2. God is one and unique.
3. God is incorporeal.
4. God is eternal.
5. Prayer is to be directed to God alone and to no other.
6. The words of the prophets are true.
7. Moses' prophecies are true, and Moses was the greatest of the prophets.
8. The Written Torah (first five books of the Bible) and Oral Torah (teachings now contained in the Talmud and other writings) were given to Moses.
9. There will be no other Torah.
10. God knows the thoughts and deeds of men.
11. God will reward the good and punish the wicked.
12. The Messiah will come.
13. The dead will be resurrected.

The Adversary

The Hebrew word for *satan* means "adversary." Jewish people believe that one of the things human beings struggle against every day is the "evil inclination." This is not a force or a being within Judaism, but rather the inherent ability to do evil in the world. Using the term *satan* to describe this evil inclination is not a general practice.

Sin is regarded in Judaism as an action undertaken by humans, not as a state of being.

SPIRITUALLY SPEAKING

"One time, when Rabban Yochanan ben Zakkai was walking in Jerusalem with Rabbi Yehosua, they arrived at where the Temple now stood in ruins. 'Woe to us,' cried Rabbi Yehosua, 'for this house where atonement was made for Israel's sins now lies in ruins!' Answered Rabban Yochanan, 'We have another, equally important source of atonement, the practice of *gemilut hasadim* ("loving kindness"), as it is stated, "I desire loving kindness and not sacrifice."'"

—*Midrash Avot de Rabbi Natan (Hosea 6:6)*

Jewish Scripture

The Torah is Judaism's most important book. It contains stories and commandments that teach about life and death. It contains the Ten Commandments as well as the 613 commandments (mitzvot). Jews consider the Ten Commandments to be the most important commandments in the Torah, and not all Jews follow the 613 mitzvot.

The Ten Commandments (believed by Jews to be delivered by God to the prophet Moses) can be expressed as follows:

1. I am the Lord your God.
2. You shall not recognize the gods of others in My presence.
3. You shall not take the Name of the Lord your God in vain.
4. Remember the day of Shabbat to keep it holy.
5. Honor your father and your mother.
6. You shall not murder.
7. You shall not commit adultery.
8. You shall not steal.
9. Do not give false testimony against your neighbor.
10. You shall not covet your fellow's possessions.

Jewish Worship and Prayer

Prayer is the fundamental characteristic of Jewish worship. A traditional Jewish prayer book may be used for instruction and explanation. It is called the siddur. Three daily prayers are the norm for many, with more prayers on the Sabbath day (Saturday) and Jewish holidays. Praying alone is allowed, but praying in the synagogue with at least ten adult males is considered the optimal choice.

KEY TERMS DEMYSTIFIED: **Synagogue**

A Jewish house of prayer.

Synagogue services vary in length and teachings according to the Jewish movement and customs of the community. It is common to find a cantor (a professional singer) at the synagogue who is paid to lead the congregation in prayers, which are conducted in Hebrew.

> ## KEY TERMS DEMYSTIFIED: Hebrew
>
> While Aramaic was the ancient spoken language used by Jews in Babylonia and Israel, **Hebrew** was the language used for recording written language, and it remains the formal language of liturgy for many Jews. The Torah was originally written in Hebrew.

Leaders in the Jewish Community

There are two kinds of leaders in a modern Jewish community, the rabbi and the cantor. The two roles, often misunderstood, are worth examining in depth. Let's take a look at them now.

The Rabbi

Some people believe that a rabbi is a "Jewish priest." Actually, this is not the case. A rabbi is a teacher who has been adequately educated in Jewish law and tradition. This allows him to teach and advise the community according to Jewish law. A Jewish priest (that is, a person authorized to perform sacred rituals) is technically known as a Kohen.

CAREFUL! *Do not assume rabbis are "Jewish priests." The formal role of priests—or Kohanim—in making Jewish sacrificial offerings ended once the Second Temple was destroyed in the first century CE. Yet these priests, regarded as descendants of Aaron, the brother of Moses, still maintain a ceremonial role in some Jewish denominations. Some of them have completed a course of education enabling them to become rabbis; others have not.*

Some Jewish communities do not have a rabbi. Members of the community can lead Jewish worship services.

The Cantor (Chazzan)

A cantor is the person who leads the congregation in prayer. In some communities, the rabbi serves as rabbi and also as cantor. Any person of good moral character and sufficient knowledge of the prayers can lead the prayer services. In larger communities, it is common to see a professional cantor hired for the role.

One of the cantor's duties is to teach young people to lead all or part of a Shabbat (Sabbath) service and to chant the liturgies associated with the bar mitzvah ceremony. Many cantors perform such duties as presiding at wedding ceremonies and funerals, visiting the sick, and teaching.

KEY TERMS DEMYSTIFIED: Bar Mitzvah

A coming-of-age ceremony for Jewish boys who reach their thirteenth birthday. The female equivalent is a **bat mitzvah**.

Major Jewish Denominations

The major Jewish denominations are often called "movements," a word that captures the importance of the faith's varied responses to its complex history.

In ancient times, in response to the Roman Empire's rule over Israel, the historical Jewish movements of Pharisees, Sadduccees, and Essenes emerged. In more recent centuries, modern and secular aspects of the culture of Europe and America brought about the modern movements of Conservative, Orthodox, and Reform Judaism. Contemporary movements that approach the Jewish faith from a mystical viewpoint are Hasidism and Kabbalah. Modern Jewish movements differ about how Judaism is practiced rather than on issues pertaining to theological doctrine.

Orthodox Judaism

This was simply mainstream Judaism until the Reform movement began in Germany.

Of all the Jewish movements, Orthodox is, as the name suggests, the most traditional in its practices. Orthodox Jews accept the entire Torah as the definitive guide for modern life. The phrase *Orthodox Judaism* encompasses a lot of territory,

KEY TERMS DEMYSTIFIED: Jewish Mysticism

Jewish mysticism focuses on internal spiritual revelations instead of academic understanding and reasoned-out decisions. Hasidism and Kabbalah are mystical approaches to the Jewish faith. Like monasticism in Christianity and Sufism in Islam, Jewish mysticism emphasizes inward, spiritual experiences over intellectual and rational knowledge. **Kabbalah** derives from a set of secret oral traditions that was standardized and spread during the Middle Ages in Europe. **Hasidic Judaism**, also spelled **Chasidic**, also emerged in Europe. Stressing personal piety and internalized mystical practices, this movement was a response to what was perceived as an overemphasis on legalism by the scholarly elite. Today, members of this movement are considered Orthodox.

describing (for instance) the Modern Orthodox wing that synthesizes traditional Jewish observance within the context of life as part of a secular modern society—and, on the other end of the spectrum, the Haredi (also known as "Ultra-Orthodox") wing, which includes many extremely conservative groups that emphasize, to varying degrees, things like distinctive dress and a general resistance toward integration with the rest of society. A commitment to careful observance of Jewish Law (for instance, the prohibition against kindling fire or doing any other work on the Sabbath) unites these different groups.

Orthodox Jews adhere strictly to the practices of daily worship, dietary laws (kashruth), daily and rigorous study of the Torah, separation of the genders in the synagogue, and traditional prayers and ceremonies. They tend to reject non-Orthodox Jewish conversions, marriages, and divorces if they are not performed within the bounds of Jewish law.

Reform Judaism

The Reform movement came out of Germany in the early 1800s, serving as a response to the perceived legalism of mainstream Judaism and also as a reflection of the liberal politics of the time. Considered the most liberal movement of modern Judaism, Reform Judaism initially endorsed sweeping changes—such as the movement of the Sabbath to Sundays—that the modern Reform movement has since reversed. The Reform movement's center of gravity has since shifted from continental Europe to the United Kingdom and North America.

Reform Jews believe the Torah to be the product of different human authors, whose work was then combined. As a result, they hold that traditional Jewish Law is subject to critical evaluation, and are more likely to interpret that law as a body of broad guidelines rather than as a set of binding restrictions on Jewish behavior. A progressive social tradition remains an important part of this movement. Modern Reform Jews believe that all humans were created in the image of God and consider themselves God's partners in making the world better. They embrace diversity in beliefs and practices, permit mixed seating and equal participation by both genders, and tend to be more inclusive than other Jewish movements. Within the modern Reform tradition, interfaith and gay families are likely to find an open door; women are accepted as rabbis, synagogue leaders, and cantors.

Reform Judaism is the largest Jewish denomination in the United States.

Conservative Judaism

Conservative Judaism (also known as Masorti Judaism outside the United States) is a moderate movement that tries to avoid the extremes of Orthodox and Reform Judaism. In keeping with the name, Conservative Jews want to conserve important traditional elements of Judaism while also allowing for reasonable modernization and rabbinical development.

Conservative Jews maintain that the ideas in the Torah originate with God, but were circulated and influenced by human beings. In practice, they aim for a middle ground between the Orthodox and Reform movements, believing that the Law can remain true to the core values of Judaism while taking on certain aspects of the surrounding (non-Jewish) culture. Women are allowed to be rabbis.

A fourth, significantly smaller movement, Reconstructionist Judaism, arose in the United States in the late nineteenth century. It views Judaism as an emerging, ever-adaptive religious civilization.

SPIRITUALLY SPEAKING

Rabbi Zusha used to say: "When I die and come before the heavenly court, if they ask me, 'Zusha, why were you not Abraham?' I'll say that I didn't have Abraham's intellectual abilities. If they say, 'Why were you not Moses?' I'll say I didn't have Moses' leadership abilities. For every such question, I'll have an answer. But if they say, 'Zusha, why were you not Zusha?' for that, I'll have no answer."

—Anonymous

Judaism in a Box	
Divinity	God. The concept of God in Judaism is uncompromisingly monotheistic.
Afterlife	The human soul is regarded in Judaism as immortal.
Purpose of Human Life	Beliefs vary.
Distinctive Practices and Beliefs	Jews are encouraged to attend services at the synagogue or temple regularly. The Sabbath, or Shabbat, begins on Friday night at dusk and concludes on Saturday night. Passover, Rosh Hashanah, and Hanukkah are among the holidays. The holy book is the Torah. The Talmud, a collection of commentaries upon the Torah, is a vitally important written record of early oral scholarship.
Outsiders Often Distracted by	Claims that Jesus was killed by "the Jews," which is a little like saying President Lincoln was killed by "the Americans"; Israeli-Palestinian relations; dietary laws; historical stereotypes.

Summary

- Judaism is the first recorded monotheistic religion.

- Action counts for much more than dogmatic belief within Judaism. The emphasis is on behavior rather than belief.

- The Torah is Judaism's most important book. It contains stories and commandments as well as the Ten Commandments and the 613 commandments (mitzvot).

- The Talmud, a collection of commentaries upon the Torah, is a vitally important written record of early oral scholarship.

- The major Jewish denominations are often called movements. Major modern movements include the Orthodox, Reform, and Conservative traditions.

QUIZ

1. *Orthopraxy* means
   A. "correctness in intellectual belief."
   B. "correctness in action or practice."
   C. "correctness in political affiliation."
   D. None of the above.

2. Judaism teaches that everyone, whether Jewish or non-Jewish, was created "b'tzelem Elohim," which is Hebrew for
   A. "in the image of God."
   B. "in the image of Abraham."
   C. "in the image of Moses."
   D. None of the above.

3. A rabbi is
   A. a Jewish priest.
   B. a Jewish singer of popular ballads.
   C. a teacher who has been adequately educated in Jewish law and tradition.
   D. None of the above.

4. A synagogue is
   A. a Jewish house of prayer.
   B. a political movement that arose in Germany in the 1800s.
   C. a religious text preserving early scholarly commentaries on the Torah.
   D. None of the above.

5. Kabbalah is
   A. a branch of Judaism originating in North America.
   B. a mystical expression of Judaism.
   C. a movement denying the existence of God.
   D. None of the above.

6. **A bar mitzvah is**

    A. a coming-of-age ceremony for Jewish boys who reach their thirteenth birthday.
    B. a coming-of-age ceremony for Jewish girls who reach their thirteenth birthday.
    C. a funeral ceremony.
    D. None of the above.

7. **The Orthodox movement**

    A. includes both Modern Orthodox and Haredi Jews.
    B. holds that all the Torah's requirements are general guidelines, not mandatory laws.
    C. arose in the early twentieth century.
    D. None of the above.

8. **The Reform movement**

    A. is the smallest Jewish movement in North America.
    B. can be traced back to nineteenth-century Europe.
    C. interprets the Torah as the literal word of God.
    D. None of the above.

9. **The Conservative movement**

    A. is the most traditionally based of the three contemporary Jewish movements.
    B. is the least traditionally based of the three contemporary Jewish movements.
    C. tends to strike a middle path between the Orthodox and Reform movements.
    D. None of the above.

10. **True or false: The Talmud is a collection of commentaries upon the Torah.**

chapter 11

Christianity: History and Context

This diverse faith system, united by a few core beliefs and distinguished by disparate practices that can sometimes make it seem like dozens of different religions, has more than two billion adherents.

That makes Christianity the world's largest faith. There is an irony, though: despite its massive numbers, or perhaps because of them, Christianity may well be one of the world's *least understood* faiths, in part because the history of its development over the centuries is so complex.

CHAPTER OBJECTIVES

In this chapter, you will learn about:

- Who Jesus was
- Turning points in the early history of the Christian church
- The role of the Apostle Paul
- The Great Schism of 1054
- The Protestant Reformation
- Major Christian denominations

It is difficult, probably impossible, to discuss the history of Christianity without at least briefly discussing its central belief: that God took human form for the forgiveness of sins.

Today, just as in the days of the early Christian church, most Christians hold Jesus Christ to be the fully divine, fully human Son of God who died on the cross, rose from the dead, and atoned sacrificially for the sins of those who believe in him. Christians also believe that Jesus is the foretold Messiah (savior or liberator) of the Hebrew scriptures, which are known by Christians as the Old Testament. Most of them also hold that belief in Jesus Christ is necessary to avoid hell and enter heaven, and anticipate Jesus Christ's return, also known as the Second Coming, which is associated with the Day of Judgment. These beliefs, rooted in the four Gospels of the New Testament, have defined the Christian Church—and, for much of history, have divided the world into two spheres: Christians and everyone else.

The long history of the Christian faith is a human story, a story of human trial and human triumph, of human empire and human error, of human power and human prayer. Behind it all, for two millennia, has stood the distinctive presence of Jesus of Nazareth, an itinerant Jewish preacher who lived in the eastern Mediterranean area during the time of the Roman emperor Tiberius.

The historical existence of Jesus is acknowledged by virtually all historians of antiquity, as is his execution by crucifixion under the Roman prefect Pontius Pilate. The life and teachings of Jesus are recounted in varying forms in the New Testament of the Christian Bible; scholars of history tend to distance themselves from these accounts, but believers do not.

SPIRITUALLY SPEAKING

"A man who was merely a man and said the sort of things Jesus said would not be a great moral teacher. He would either be a lunatic—on the level with the man who says he is a poached egg—or else he would be the Devil of Hell. You must make your choice. Either this man was, and is, the Son of God, or else a madman or something worse. You can shut him up for a fool, you can spit at him and kill him as a demon or you can fall at his feet and call him Lord and God, but let us not come with any patronizing nonsense about his being a great human teacher. He has not left that open to us. He did not intend to."

—*C. S. Lewis*, Mere Christianity

The massive *Christ the Redeemer* statue in Rio de Janeiro, Brazil.

Credit: © McGraw-Hill Education/Barry Barker, Photographer

The Apostolic Period

In its infancy, Christianity was an offshoot of Judaism in the Roman-controlled Levant region now known by Christians as the Holy Land, starting roughly in the middle of the first century CE. The early Church was under the leadership of the Apostles of Christ during what is now known as the apostolic period.

KEY TERMS DEMYSTIFIED: **Apostle**

A Greek word meaning "emissary." The term may be taken to mean one of the original Jewish followers of Jesus commissioned to spread the good news of his ministry (among whom were Simon Peter, the "rock" on which Jesus proclaimed that the Church would be built, and John, the "disciple whom Jesus loved"). The word may also be used to include later converts such as Paul of Tarsus, the "apostle to the Gentiles" (Romans 11:13).

The apostolic period's history is recorded in the books of the New Testament. It is during this span of time that the Apostles, notably Paul, a former persecutor of Christians, helped to spread the teachings of the early Church and worked tirelessly to establish small communities of Christians both within and outside the Roman Empire. During this time, Christians often faced severe persecution, including torture and execution, from political and religious authorities.

The Apostle Paul was the most successful Christian missionary of the first-century world. He founded Christian churches in Asia Minor and Europe, and skillfully used his status as a Jew and a citizen of the Roman Empire to support his ministry. Paul claimed a special commission from the resurrected Jesus Christ, received in a vision.

In the early years of the Christian Church, believers often faced relentless opposition. Christians were officially blamed by Roman Emperor Nero for the Great Fire of Rome in 64 CE, and subsequently many official Roman policies suppressed the religion.

Christianity's identity as a separate religion rather than a sect of Judaism was a major issue, both internally and externally. Early Christians often worshiped in synagogues, and though Jewish leaders denied any Messiah had come, the split between the two faiths was not sudden. The apostolic period also saw the writing of most of the major early Christian spiritual texts.

Christianity spread during this period despite Roman persecution, largely through its commitment to humanitarian works and an accessible set of beliefs and practices, both of which appealed to the poorer classes of Roman society.

The Ante-Nicene Period

After the turn of the first century of the Common Era, the apostolic period ended, and Christianity entered a new phase that would come to be known as the Ante-Nicene period. (The name means "before the Council of Nicea," about which more in a moment.)

This was a critical period of consolidation and growth. Christianity spread slowly, the early Christian canon emerged, and various teachings regarded as heretical by Church leaders were condemned and abandoned. The end of this period also marked a major turning point for the faith, one that could hardly have been predicted during the dark days of the reign of Nero: the official end of Roman persecution of Christianity. This occurred in the early fourth century, when the emperor Constantine I personally embraced Christianity (though the details on when and how that occurred are murky) and then issued the Edict of Milan in 313 CE. This proclamation officially legalized Christianity within the Roman Empire.

The Edict of Toleration resulted from a meeting in 313 CE between Emperor Constantine, ruler of the Western Roman Empire, and his colleague and rival Lucinius, who held sway in the East. The two agreed to treat Christians (and other religious minorities) with tolerance. Contrary to popular belief, the Edict of Toleration did not establish Christianity as the official state religion of the Empire; that would not take place for the better part of a century. The Edict of Toleration is important, however, because it reflected Constantine's own Christianity and because it ended official persecution of Christians by the Roman government.

The First Council of Nicea

Constantine convened what is now known as the First Council of Nicaea in 325, in present-day Turkey. This gathering of Christian bishops marked another turning point in Christian history. The initial business of the council was to address the challenge of what is now known as the Arian heresy: a popular early Church leader named Arius taught that, rather than being one with God the Father, Jesus the Son of God was a separate entity created from nothing. The contention this doctrine caused within the church led to Arius's excommunication and to the formulation of the now-famous Nicene Creed, which established the formal Trinitarian doctrine of Christianity, which regards God the Father, God the Son, and God the Holy Spirit as Divine.

The First Council of Nicaea was important because it was the first formulation of an overarching Christian orthodoxy. This increased Christianity's influence and unity. The Nicene Creed was originally formulated in 325 CE, and revised in 381 CE at the Council of Constantinople.

SPIRITUALLY SPEAKING

"I believe in one God, the Father Almighty, Maker of heaven and earth, and of all things visible and invisible, and in one Lord Jesus Christ, the only-begotten Son of God, begotten of the Father before all worlds; God of God, Light of Light, very God of very God; begotten, not made, being of one substance with the Father, by whom all things were made. Who, for us men for our salvation, came down from heaven, and was incarnate by the Holy Spirit of the virgin Mary, and was made man; and was crucified also for us under Pontius Pilate; He suffered and was buried; and the third day He rose again, according to the Scriptures; and ascended into heaven, and sits on the right hand of the Father; and He shall come again, with glory, to judge the quick and the dead; whose kingdom shall have no end. And I believe in the Holy Ghost, the Lord and Giver of Life; who proceeds from the Father; who with the Father and the Son together is worshipped and glorified; who spoke by the prophets. And I believe one holy catholic and apostolic Church. I acknowledge one baptism for the remission of sins; and I look for the resurrection of the dead, and the life of the world to come. Amen."

—*Nicene Creed, 381 CE*

The Middle Ages and the Crusades

By 380 CE, Christianity had become the official religion of the Roman Empire by Imperial decree, and five separate centers of Christian organization, called Sees, had been established: Rome, Constantinople, Antioch, Jerusalem, and Alexandria.

After the fall of the Western Roman Empire in 476, the Christian Church became a major center of culture and stability in the lives of Western Europeans. During the Early Medieval period that followed the empire's fall, political organization was often violent and unstable, and the Church came to be seen as an important point of stability. The actual papacy of Rome was not always seen as dominant in this period, and other western bishops were often more influential as spiritual leaders.

During this time, Christian missionaries spread across Europe, reaching as far as Anglo-Saxon Britain and Ireland. Monasteries became a characteristic part of Christian life and organization during this time as well, providing havens for spiritual and academic learning, as well as wielding significant political influence. In the Eastern Roman Empire, the Eastern Patriarchy was closely tied to the Emperor at Constantinople, and the two both held significant power over the people of the Empire.

Then—an earthquake. Seemingly out of nowhere, Islam arose from Arabia and began to rise dramatically in religious, political, and social influence, starting in the seventh century CE. The centuries that followed were contentious, eventful, and divisive ones for the Christian faith.

In the startlingly new environment, a rift was deepening. The sharply differing views of the Sees of Constantinople and Rome on a wide range of issues grew more and more serious. Those disagreements would eventually reach a head, and would lead to the establishment of the Roman Catholic and Eastern Orthodox Churches as separate entities, in a split known as the Great Schism of 1054. Up to this point, there had been only one "catholic" (that is to say, "universal") Church.

KEY TERMS DEMYSTIFIED: Great Schism of 1054

The culmination of a series of disagreements over authority on a number of complex religious and political issues. It led the Roman Church to excommunicate the Eastern Patriarchy, and vice versa. Prior to the schism, the Eastern and Western strands of the Christian faith had been different but had generally had cordial relations. After it, the two Churches formally accused each other of heresy.

Problems with Islam intensified and worsened the split. In 1072 the Egyptian-based Fatmids lost control of Palestine to the emergent Seljuq Empire of Turkey. Both empires were Muslim, but the Fatmids and their predecessors had generally been amenable to and tolerant of Christian pilgrimages to the Holy Land. The Seljuqs initially were less tolerant and discriminated against Christians in the

Holy Land for a brief period of time. This, combined with the Seljuqs' general expansionism, led the political and military leaders of the Eastern Roman Empire to a grave concern. In 1095 the Eastern Empire appealed to the Roman Catholic Church to send military aid, and the Pope responded at the Council of Clermont with a campaign to persuade European royalty to commit to retaking the Holy Land. They did, and in so doing they launched the brutal series of wars known as the Crusades.

CAREFUL! *Use of the word* crusade *in a positive context may offend some non-Christians.*

The Crusades were a complex series of military and religious expeditions that took place from the eleventh to the early fourteenth centuries CE. Most of them were waged against Muslims and had the goal of establishing Christian kingdoms in the Holy Land; several campaigns ended up targeting other places, including northern Africa, Egypt, and Turkey. The Crusades were not unified in command, and often they were considered pilgrimages that secured immediate entry to heaven for Crusaders who died in battle. The outcomes of the campaigns varied wildly; in the end, all the Christian strongholds in the Middle East fell. A major outcome of the bloody struggles, however, was an increase of power and influence of the Catholic Church.

After the fall of the Byzantine Empire to the Ottoman Empire in 1453, the seat of the Eastern Orthodox Church moved to Russia, where the Orthodox faith remains strong today. It is today the dominant system of belief among religious practitioners in Russia, as well as in Belarus, Bulgaria, Cyprus, Georgia, Greece, Macedonia, Moldova, Montenegro, Romania, Serbia, and Ukraine. There are minority groups of Orthodox Christians in Jordan, Israel, Lebanon, and Syria.

The Protestant Reformation

After the Crusades, the Catholic Church wielded great power in Europe. The Church's unquestioned authority on spiritual matters led many to conclude that corruption, excess, and inaccessibility were serious challenges within the Church. Of particular concern was the practice of granting indulgences, which were state-ments of temporal forgiveness that absolved the holder of punishment for a sin— often, in return for a monetary donation.

Combined with other issues, this dispute over indulgences divided the Church. Following a period of unrest called the Western Schism from 1378 to 1416, during which time two different men claimed to be Pope, there were a few prominent voices calling for reform. Most notable were Jan Hus of the University of Prague and John Wycliffe of Oxford University, who denounced many practices of the Church, particularly indulgences. Though the Church did convene a council to discuss the issue, the two men were eventually burned as heretics, Wycliffe posthumously.

The impassioned debate over the perceived problems of doctrine, ethics, authority, practice, and structure within the Catholic Church took many forms and played out in many arenas. That debate did not solely concern itself with the controversial practice of granting indulgences; other important protests focused on objections to the spiritual authority of the Pope; on the use of Latin, generally spoken only by the wealthy and the learned, in religious services; on the vast disparity of wealth between laypeople and senior religious figures; and on the sexual immorality of many supposedly celibate members of the clergy, up to and including the very highest. (Pope Alexander VI, for instance, was known to have fathered seven children.)

KEY TERMS DEMYSTIFIED: **Pope**

The Bishop of Rome and the global leader of the Catholic Church.

Matters came to a head in 1517, when a monk named Martin Luther wrote 95 theses, or scholarly arguments, condemning various Church practices. Although Luther is perhaps most famous for nailing these arguments to a church door in Wittenberg, Germany, it is probably more significant that his arguments were eventually translated from the academic language of Latin into German and circulated by means of a new technology: the printing press with movable type.

Luther's arguments earned him fame, won him excommunication from the Roman Catholic Church, and sparked the open movement against the papacy that is now called the Protestant Reformation. Luther and other protesters explicitly broke from the theology of the Catholic Church, arguing that salvation did not come from the Church as a system but instead from individual faith in Jesus.

Many separate movements and doctrines emerged from this larger movement, but the two most visible teachers of the Reformation were Luther and John Calvin, and eventually the two largest branches of Reformation thought became known as Lutheranism and Calvinism.

The Roman Catholic Church initially condemned the Protestant Reformation, but the movement's growth and influence would not allow it to go without a larger response. The Catholic Church then began a Counter-Reformation with the Council of Trent, from 1545 to 1563. This movement attempted to reemphasize the spirituality of the Catholic Church, and although it firmly upheld the general structure of the Catholic Church and the authority of the Pope, it did bring some important changes to the institution. It increased the education available to priests and lessened the distance between the clergy and laypeople. The main religious statement of the Counter-Reformation was a reiteration of the importance of earthly works and good deeds to accompany individual faith, in contrast to the Protestant assertion that faith alone determined salvation.

Divisions over the Reformation

Europe was bitterly divided by the Protestant Reformation, and many long-reaching conflicts arose from the movement. France and the Germanic states of the Holy Roman Empire were deeply divided between Protestants and Catholics, leading to a series of religiously motivated civil and foreign wars, including the bloody Thirty Years' War. King Henry VIII of England founded the Church of England in 1536, installing himself as the head of that Church and beginning the tradition known as Anglicanism. The interaction of the ruling Protestant English and the largely Catholic native population of Ireland would lead to centuries of strife.

In addition, there was a sizeable minority group called the Puritans operating across many countries, particularly in England. They felt that the politically supported churches, too, were in need of reform. Many of them emigrated to what would become the American Colonies to avoid persecution, eventually founding the Congregationalist movement.

A distinctive and diverse Unitarian movement arose in the eighteenth century, understanding God as a single entity and holding Jesus Christ to be a "son" of God in a metaphorical sense, but not divine in any personal sense. This movement, perhaps the most open-ended in Christian theology, has taken many forms.

Unitarians consider Jesus to have been a prophet and reject the mainstream doctrine of Trinitarianism, as well as other seemingly central principles of conventional Christianity (such as the inherent authority of the Bible).

Major Branches of Christianity After the Protestant Reformation

In modern common parlance, the term *Protestant* is used as a convenient catch-all term to describe Christian churches that do not recognize the authority of either the Catholic Church or the Eastern Orthodox Church. It's important to note that there are many divergent Christian denominations that do not follow either of these churches, and that the *Protestant* label, like all umbrella terms, is prone to overuse and oversimplification. Following is a summary of some of the important Christian religious movements that emerged after the Protestant Reformation.

The Anglican Church, consisting of the Church of England and its affiliates, is one of the larger branches. Founded by Henry VIII and solidified by Elizabeth I, the Anglican Church is often considered a middle ground between the Catholic Church and other Protestant traditions, maintaining many Catholic-style organizational structures and theological elements while incorporating several important Protestant ideas and considering itself distinct from the authority of the Roman papacy. A unique element of the Anglican faith is the Common Book of Prayer, which describes the structures of Anglican worship services. Churches that consider themselves part of the See of Canterbury, and under the authority of the Archbishop of Canterbury, are part of the Anglican umbrella, including the Episcopal Church in the United States. Anglican denominations are common in areas that were once under the rule of the British Empire. The Anglican tradition was and remains an important part of the British identity.

Lutheranism, like Anglicanism, stems directly from the Reformation, following the original ideas of Martin Luther. The Lutheran Church maintains many of the traditions and ideas of the Catholic Church before the Reformation but places emphasis on the concept that faith in God's Word is the only path to salvation, rather than the Catholic idea of both faith and deeds being important. The Lutheran Church also emphasizes the teachings of the early Church Fathers and the importance of the Eucharist, in which the real presence of Christ is assumed. The Lutheran faith is historically strong in Northern Europe and Scandinavia.

There are many different denominations of Calvinist or Reformed Christianity, one of the largest of which is the Presbyterian Church. It is defined partly by its adherence to an organizational scheme involving presbyters, in which each individual church is governed by an elected body of elders, and in turn governed by a hierarchy of similar elected councils. The Presbyterian Church, and Calvinist-based Reformed churches in general, do not accept the doctrine of transubstantiation by which the Communion meal is held to become the literal body of Jesus Christ. This is one of the main differences between the Presbyterian and Lutheran Churches. The Presbyterian Church is historically strong in Scotland. Similar to Presbyterianism is Congregationalism, another reformed branch of Christianity; its practitioners trace its history back to the Puritans. Congregationalists are defined by their locally autonomous organizational structure, in which the congregation of each individual church governs its own affairs. Congregationalist Churches are common in places where Puritans settled, particularly New England.

The Methodist Church is one part of a larger Evangelical Christian tradition. It traces its founding to the preaching of John Wesley. Methodists put their focus on the charitable, community aspects of Christianity and the missionary message of Christ, seeking to spread Christianity's message. Methodism has its roots in an Anglican reform movement, and many Methodists are connected to the Episcopal or Anglican Churches, although it is generally considered a separate denomination.

The Baptist Church, a large American denomination, was founded in the teachings of John Smyth. Baptist Churches place emphasis on the importance of baptism to faith, and in particular reject the idea of infant baptism. Instead, they practice "believer's baptisms" of adults, who use the ritual as an affirmation of their faith and devotion. Both of these traditions were spread widely in the United States by the populist religious movements known as the First and Second Great Awakenings, and are particularly prevalent in the American South.

Many other unique Christian faith traditions have developed in the years since the Reformation. Some are not considered to fall into the Protestant grouping. Among these is the Seventh-day Adventist Church, which was founded in the mid-1800s. The Seventh-day Adventists consider Saturday rather than Sunday to be the Sabbath; another important aspect of their doctrine is the imminent Second Coming of Christ, which believers must be prepared for, because God is currently in the process of judging humanity. The Seventh-day Adventists also have a unique conception of the afterlife, believing that rather than immediately being judged for heaven or hell upon death, human souls instead are unconscious upon dying and are then awoken on Judgment Day.

The Mormon Church, also known as the Church of Jesus Christ of Latter-day Saints, was also founded in America in the nineteenth century, and has its own set of unique beliefs. Alongside the Bible, Mormons hold the Book of Mormon as a Holy Book, believing it to have been handed down by God to their founder, Joseph Smith. This book details the lives of several prophets not told of in the Bible, many of whom lived in what would become America. There are several distinct branches of Mormonism, which differ on ideas such as baptism for the dead, plural marriage, and the acceptance of the Trinity. Mormonism is as much a cultural identity as a religious one. Jesus Christ is the central figure in Mormonism, and Mormons self-identify as Christians, though the many unique aspects of their theology have led to controversy and persecution.

The Jehovah's Witnesses are another Christian sect with unique beliefs and practices, founded in the late 1870s. Their faith is based on a strict interpretation of the Bible that warns of a coming Armageddon. They reject notions such as the Trinity and the immortality of the soul and consider society to be enmeshed in sin, and their faith is termed "the truth." They do not observe many mainstream Christian holidays and rituals, including Easter and Christmas, because they consider them to be rooted in pagan tradition, and they limit their interaction with people outside of their faith. They are also highly active as missionaries, seeking converts in order to build God's Kingdom on earth.

Summary

- Christianity, a diverse global faith, claims more than two billion adherents.

- Christianity began as a movement within Judaism. First-century believers faced intense persecution. The Apostle Paul established a number of Christian churches that appealed to Gentiles (non-Jews).

- A rift between the Christian churches based in Rome and Constantinople led to the Great Schism of 1054, forming two branches of the faith now known as Catholicism and Orthodox Christianity.

- The Roman Catholic Church helped to lead the Crusades, a long series of religious wars against Islamic forces that did not succeed in reclaiming the

Holy Land but made the Church an extremely powerful European social institution.

- Complaints about corruption and doctrinal problems within the Roman Catholic Church led to a series of reform efforts. Early reformers were executed, but Martin Luther's reform movement in early sixteenth-century Germany sparked what is now known as the Protestant Reformation.

- Multiple strands of distinctive Christian practice and belief emerged in Europe and elsewhere following the Protestant Reformation.

QUIZ

1. **Jesus was an**

   A. itinerant Jewish preacher.

   B. Egyptian mystic who posed as an agnostic.

   C. early Roman pagan who converted to Judaism.

   D. None of the above.

2. **The historical existence of Jesus is**

   A. disputed by responsible scholars.

   B. acknowledged by virtually all historians of antiquity.

   C. only acknowledged by Christians.

   D. None of the above.

3. **The Apostle Paul was**

   A. Jewish.

   B. Gentile.

   C. an atheist.

   D. None of the above.

4. **According to the Nicene Creed, Christians believe that Jesus**

   A. is not God.

   B. is not a human being.

   C. is part of a divine Trinity that includes God the Father, God the Son, and God the Holy Spirit.

   D. None of the above.

5. **The Great Schism of 1054 involved**

   A. the Sees of Rome and Constantinople.

   B. Martin Luther and Pope Andrew VI.

   C. the Roman Empire and the Levant.

   D. None of the above.

6. **The branch of Christianity formerly headquartered in Constantinople is now known as**

   A. the Unitarian Church.

   B. the Eastern Orthodox Church.

   C. the Church of Jesus Christ of Latter-day Saints.

   D. None of the above.

7. **After the Crusades**

   A. the Roman Catholic Church had even greater influence and authority in Europe.

   B. the Roman Catholic Church had less influence and authority in Europe than at any point in its history.

   C. the Roman Catholic Church was officially disbanded.

   D. None of the above.

8. **The Protestant movement arose in part out of disputes over**

   A. which of the Gospels was the oldest and most authentic reflection of the teachings of Jesus.

   B. the nature of Jesus.

   C. the granting of indulgences by Catholic clergy, which were held to forgive sins.

   D. None of the above.

9. **The Pope is**

   A. the bishop of Rome and the global leader of the world's Roman Catholics.

   B. the second-in-command in terms of leadership of the Catholic Church.

   C. holder of an office established in the early twentieth century.

   D. None of the above.

10. **The Anglican Church**

    A. accepts the authority of the Roman Catholic Church.

    B. rejects the authority of the Roman Catholic Church.

    C. has no position on the authority of the Roman Catholic Church.

    D. None of the above.

Christianity: Core Beliefs and Practices

What articles of faith and observances define Christian religious practice? When you complete this chapter, you will be able to describe the core beliefs of most Christians and spiritual practices, rituals, and holidays within the diverse global faith of Christianity.

CHAPTER OBJECTIVES

In this chapter, you will learn about:

- What *most* Christians believe
- What *most* Christians practice
- Major Christian holidays

What do Christians believe? There are some broadly accepted answers to that simple-sounding question—and some longstanding disagreements, as well.

For instance, the question of what will take place in the lives of devout Christians who are alive on earth in the period before the Second Coming of Christ receives different answers from different denominations. Some Christians (notably Roman Catholics, Orthodox Christians, and Lutherans) believe in a general final resurrection, when Christ returns a single time. Others (mostly from American denominations) believe that a group of believers will literally ascend to "meet the Lord in the air," and thus escape a difficult Tribulation period that must be endured by others left on earth.

In fact, there is a wide range of intricately competitive views on the timing of Christ's return, and an equally complex array of opinions on such issues as whether that return will occur in one event or two, and what exactly will happen to the faithful when it does take place. This topic, like so many in Christianity, is impossible to summarize concisely in a way that adequately reflects the beliefs of the many denominations involved.

Why mention this here? Because the answers you hear when you ask "what Christians believe" about certain topics or "what Christians do" in terms of worship can be quite tricky—for at least three reasons. First, the responses depend largely on whom you ask and how you ask. Second, the answers often don't give you much information that is relevant to *most* Christian practice and belief. Third, the answers may point you toward differences rather than commonalities—and the commonalities are, as a rule, much more important to Christian belief than the differences.

These three problems, taken together, tend to do more to *mystify* Christianity for outsiders than demystify it.

What Do *Most* Christians Believe?

As you may have gathered by now, separating the essence of "Christian belief" from the faith's own historical discussions can be a complicated business. Yet there are certain core beliefs that have stood the test of time. You encountered some of them in the previous chapter.

Core Beliefs

A complex of core beliefs, powerfully influenced by both the Gospel accounts of Jesus's ministry and the Second Nicene Creed, are accepted by most contemporary Christians. Look at them again:

Most Christians hold Jesus Christ to be the fully divine, fully human Son of God who died on the cross, rose from the dead, and atones sacrificially for the sins of those who believe in him. Christians also believe that Jesus is the foretold Messiah (savior or liberator) of the Hebrew scriptures, which are known by Christians as the Old Testament. Most of them also hold that belief in Jesus Christ is necessary to avoid hell and enter heaven, and anticipate Jesus Christ's return, also known as the Second Coming, which is associated with the Day of Judgment.

If we add to this the doctrine of the Trinity—held to be implied by certain key Gospel passages—and you have a foundation structure on which most, but not all, people who self-identify as Christians find common ground.

KEY TERMS DEMYSTIFIED: Trinity

An important doctrine of mainstream Christianity identifying "one God in three persons"—God the Father, God the Son, and God the Holy Spirit. Most, but not all, Christians accept the doctrine of the Trinity.

Let's look at some other important commonalities of belief among Christians.

Monotheism

A central tenet of Christianity is the belief that there is one singular, supreme God, who is omniscient, omnipotent, and omnipresent. Like the other Abrahamic belief systems, Judaism and Islam, Christianity teaches that there are no other deities than the one true God, who created the universe.

CAREFUL! *Christians regard their faith as monotheistic. For most of them, the doctrine of the Trinity is not seen as an obstacle to that belief. Some branches of Christianity disagree, and distance themselves from Trinitarian formulations, but the majority of the faithful see no conflict whatsoever between belief in the One God of the Hebrew scriptures and belief in the "Father, Son, and Holy Spirit."*

Faith in the Teachings of Jesus

Reverence for and obedience to the teachings of Jesus Christ is another "nonnegotiable" of the Christian faith. To be sure, interpreting and summarizing those teachings definitively sometimes proved a challenging, divisive task for Christian believers.

There are any number of touchy questions on which there is no universal consensus on what Jesus taught. Still, most Christians would agree that Jesus's ministry did teach a powerful message of redemption, tolerance, love for humanity, and obedience to God. Most would also agree that attempting to follow that guidance is an essential part of being a Christian.

No Christianity that excludes the teachings of Jesus can be considered complete. The greatest Christian thinkers—from St. Augustine to C. S. Lewis to Mother Teresa—have all emphasized the importance of returning to the Gospel message for personal guidance. Among the most celebrated and powerful words attributed to Jesus are the Beatitudes, which begin the account of the Sermon on the Mount that is found in the Gospel of Matthew.

SPIRITUALLY SPEAKING

"Blessed are the poor in spirit: for theirs is the kingdom of heaven. Blessed are they that mourn: for they shall be comforted. Blessed are the meek: for they shall inherit the earth. Blessed are they which do hunger and thirst after righteousness: for they shall be filled. Blessed are the merciful: for they shall obtain mercy. Blessed are the pure in heart: for they shall see God. Blessed are the peacemakers: for they shall be called the children of God. Blessed are they which are persecuted for righteousness' sake: for theirs is the kingdom of heaven. Blessed are ye, when men shall revile you, and persecute you, and shall say all manner of evil against you falsely, for my sake. Rejoice, and be exceeding glad: for great is your reward in heaven: for so persecuted they the prophets which were before you."

—*Matthew 5:3–12*

A Word About Saints

In the language of the New Testament, this term *saint* is generally translated to mean a committed and faithful believer in God. Among certain denominations, particularly the Roman Catholic and Eastern Orthodox Churches, *saint* is a formal title indicating a mortal individual with a special relationship to God, allowing him or her to perform miracles and receive prayers after his or her death, and it must be conferred by the Church. Other denominations use the term to mean any follower of Christ who truly believes, and may treat *saint* as a term of recognition and camaraderie among living members of the church. Still other denominations avoid the term altogether.

What Do *Most* Christians Practice?

There are a number of important common elements to mainstream Christian worship. These include the following.

Communion

One of the most important rituals in Christianity is Communion, or Eucharist. This rite mirrors accounts of the Last Supper, an important event described in the Gospels where Jesus spoke to his disciples before his arrest and eventual execution, then ritually enacted his own forthcoming sacrifice using bread and wine. Communion's specifics vary from sect to sect but generally consist of eating special bread, meant to represent the Body of Christ, and drinking special wine, meant to represent the Blood of Christ.

The Communion meal is meant to commemorate the sacrifice Jesus made for humanity, and is a powerful symbol of salvation. Some denominations, particularly the Catholic Church, take the symbolism of the rite literally, believing in the miracle of Transubstantiation, whereby the bread and wine literally and miraculously become the blood and body of Christ during the Eucharist. Other denominations view this rite as primarily metaphorical.

Weekly Services

Communion is usually a central element of weekly communal worship services. The modern Christian Sabbath is Sunday, regarded as the day of Christ's resurrection after having been crucified.

"And on the day called Sunday, all who live in cities or in the country gather together to one place, and the memoirs of the apostles or the writings of the prophets are read, as long as time permits; then, when the reader has ceased, the president verbally instructs, and exhorts to the imitation of these good things. Then we all rise together and pray, and, as we before said, when our prayer is ended, bread and wine and water are brought, and the president in like manner offers prayers and thanksgivings, according to his ability, and the people assent, saying Amen; and there is a distribution to each, and a participation of that over which thanks have been given, and to those who are absent a portion is sent by the deacons. And they who are well to do, and willing, give what each thinks fit; and what is collected is deposited with the president, who succors the orphans and widows and those who, through sickness or any other cause, are in want, and those who are in bonds and the strangers sojourning among us, and in a word takes care of all who are in need."

—*Justin Martyr, second-century Christian*

Prayer

Prayer, alone or in a group, is another essential part of the Christian faith. Prayer is seen as a way of communing with God to strengthen belief, receive forgiveness, and obtain guidance for leading a righteous life.

"When we pray for the Spirit's help . . . we will simply fall down at the Lord's feet in our weakness. There we will find the victory and power that comes from His love."

—*Andrew Murray, South African writer and Christian pastor*

Prayer takes many forms in Christianity. Prayer can be highly ritualized, or experienced as deeply personal and spontaneous process of communication with God, with no formal guidelines.

Important prayers within Christian tradition include the Lord's Prayer, which the Gospels inform us was passed directly from Jesus to the disciples.

SPIRITUALLY SPEAKING

"Our Father which art in heaven, Hallowed be thy name. Thy kingdom come, Thy will be done in earth, as it is in heaven. Give us this day our daily bread. And forgive us our debts, as we forgive our debtors. And lead us not into temptation, but deliver us from evil: For thine is the kingdom, and the power, and the glory, for ever. Amen."

—*The Lord's Prayer (Matthew 6:9–13)*

Baptism

Another ritual important to Christianity is the tradition of baptism, by which a person is inducted into the Church by being specially anointed in a ceremony using water. Like Communion, the interpretation and specifics of this ritual can vary greatly from sect to sect. Whether this ritual should be performed soon after an infant's birth or as a rite of passage after individuals reach an age at which they can agree to it, as well as the ritual's relation to an individual's salvation, are the main points of difference, though the actual process of baptism can also differ.

The Church: Fellowship with Other Christian Believers

The Church is an important term to Christians, representing as it does the community of believers acting as God's vehicle on earth. Again, the specifics of interpretation differ, but generally *the Church* is accepted to mean both a physical building where believers gather, as well as the spiritual and organizational connection between those believers through which the Holy Spirit works. The word *fellowship*—derived from the Book of Acts in the Bible—is taken to mean a communal gathering of like-minded Christians.

Major Christian Holidays

Some Christian denominations follow a strict, detailed liturgical calendar; others do not. The following holidays are considered central to Christian observance by many believers.

- **Lent.** A forty-day period preceding Easter that emphasizes self-examination and self-denial.
- **Palm Sunday.** This holiday celebrates Jesus's entry into Jerusalem. A springtime holiday, it is generally observed in early April. Western and Eastern Christian Churches take differing approaches to setting the date.
- **Good Friday.** This holiday observes the day when Jesus was crucified.
- **Easter.** The most important Christian holiday, this holiday celebrates the resurrection of Jesus.
- **Pentecost.** Celebrated 40 days after Easter, this holiday celebrates the coming of the Holy Spirit.
- **Advent.** The four Sundays before Christmas, devoted to preparation for that holiday and for the Second Coming of Christ.
- **Christmas.** Observed on December 25, this holiday celebrates the birth of Jesus.

Christianity in a Box	
Divinity	Most Christians worship a Triune God (Father, Son, and Holy Spirit), regarded as identical to the God of the Hebrew scriptures.
Afterlife	Eternal heaven or eternal hell. Some Christians believe in a realm known as purgatory where sins may be expiated.
Purpose of Human Life	Atonement through Christ, the Son of God.
Distinctive Practices and Beliefs	Most Christians take part in Sunday worship services. The holy scripture is the Bible, divided into Old and New Testaments. The Old Testament corresponds with the traditional Hebrew scriptures; the New Testament features four canonically accepted Gospels and numerous other books, including letters attributed to important early figures in the Christian Church.
Outsiders Often Distracted by	Communion. Predictions concerning the Day of Judgment.

Summary

- Most Christians hold Jesus Christ to be the fully divine, fully human Son of God who died on the cross, rose from the dead, and atones sacrificially for the sins of those who believe in him. Christians also believe that Jesus is the foretold Messiah (savior or liberator) of the Hebrew scriptures, which are known by Christians as the Old Testament.

- Most Christians also hold that belief in Jesus Christ is necessary to avoid hell and enter heaven, and anticipate Jesus Christ's return, also known as the Second Coming, which is associated with the Day of Judgment.

- In addition, most, but not all, Christians accept the doctrine of the Trinity, which identifies "one God in three persons"—God the Father, God the Son, and God the Holy Spirit.

QUIZ

1. **The Trinity is**
   A. a doctrine emphasizing the common elements of the three faiths of Judaism, Christianity, and Islam.
   B. a doctrine emphasizing the special status of the three disciples closest to Jesus.
   C. an important doctrine of mainstream Christianity identifying "one God in three persons."
   D. None of the above.

2. **The Sermon on the Mount appears in**
   A. the Gospels.
   B. the Old Testament.
   C. the Book of Acts.
   D. None of the above.

3. **Communion is**
   A. an outreach program to non-Christians.
   B. an Easter garment.
   C. a rite mirroring accounts of the Last Supper.
   D. None of the above.

4. **For most Christians, the Sabbath is**
   A. Sunday.
   B. Saturday.
   C. Friday.
   D. None of the above.

5. **Baptism is**
   A. a practice condemned by most Christian denominations.
   B. an important rite of Christianity by which a person is inducted into the church by being specially anointed in a ceremony using water.
   C. a rite held during a Christian funeral service.
   D. None of the above.

6. **A popular translation of the Lord's Prayer begins with the words**

    A. "Our Father, which art in Heaven."

    B. "Blessed are the poor."

    C. "Give us this day our daily bread."

    D. None of the above.

7. **Good Friday is**

    A. a celebration of the coming of the Holy Spirit.

    B. a celebration of the birth of Jesus.

    C. a celebration of Jesus's resurrection from the dead.

    D. None of the above.

8. **The most important holiday on the Christian calendar is**

    A. Lent.

    B. Easter.

    C. Christmas.

    D. None of the above.

9. **True or false: Christians agree unanimously on the details of the anticipated Second Coming of Christ.**

10. **True or false: Christians universally accept the doctrine of the Trinity.**

chapter **13**

Islam: History and Context

Near the end of the sixth century CE, an epoch-making religious figure, Muhammad the Prophet of Islam, was born in Arabia. The life and teachings of this man heralded the advent of Islam in history. The long debate over the origin, significance, and legacy of this man's mission has often produced more confusion than understanding—and has made demystifying Islam a formidable task.

In this chapter we undertake that task by examining the history and context of this global faith, whose non-Arab adherents now form a sizeable majority among its 1.5 billion followers.

CHAPTER OBJECTIVES

In this chapter, you will learn about:

- Who Muhammad was
- The main events of Muhammad's life and mission
- What the word *Islam* means
- What factors connect Islam to other faiths

Muslims do not regard Islam as a new religion. For them it is rather the purification and reconstitution of the unique monotheistic faith that God provided for humankind from the very beginning. And this is one of the keys to demystifying Islam: It is regarded by its adherents as the *eternal* religion, the culmination of a series of divine communications to humanity.

Countless prophets in history, Muslims believe, have shared a common objective: to preach the divinity of a transcendent Creator to their own peoples. In Islamic thought, this line of prophecy culminated in the Arabian Prophet Muhammad, whose mission is held to extend not to a narrow tribe or even to a nation, but to the entire world.

KEY TERMS DEMYSTIFIED: Islam

Originating from the Arabic root S-L-M, which means roughly "to be safe and free." The infinitive for *Islam* means both "to surrender" and "to be unfettered." For this reason the person who "surrenders" is called a Muslim—the active participle of *Islam*—for submitting to the will of God.

We move on to the universality of Islam, which is a central component of Islamic belief. The Islamic tradition declares that throughout history all the prophets, sages, and persons of wisdom have taught humanity the same essential message: to "surrender" to God. In this sense, Muhammad's mission is regarded as a confirmation of the teachings of previous prophets.

Islam and the Middle East

Arabia is the crucible of Islam, and it forms part of a larger religious context. Mesopotamia, sometimes called the Near East, is the region in which the Judeo-Christian family of religions first flourished. The origins and content of Islam cannot be viewed in isolation from the religious history of Judaism and Christianity, which also have their roots in the Near East. Muslims regard Jews and Christians as "People of the Book," and as meriting special tolerance given their acknowledgment of the God of Abraham as the one true God.

Though different in orientation, the three religions share certain basic features. All three are transcendental, holding that beyond this life there is a higher world, the realm of the divine, which can be attained through ethical action and faith in

God; each one claims a monotheistic deity; and each is universal, believing that one God created and continues to govern the whole universe and all people.

Mecca

The center of the new religion that arose in seventh-century Arabia was Mecca. This was both the commercial center and the capital of the pre-Islamic religion and its pagan cults. Its Ka`ba (literally, "the cube"), a rectangular stone building surrounded by holy space associated with Abraham, formed the point of the annual pilgrimage for the whole of Arabia. Mecca had the added attraction of hosting the fair of Ukaz, which coincided with the annual pilgrimage to the Meccan shrine. These activities were of immense political, economic, and cultural importance to the prestige of the city.

At the time that Islam emerged, major changes were taking place in the political economy of Arabia. Under the impact of commercial development and commodity trade, the nomadic way of life, based on kinship in a barter economy, was giving way to a more settled society, characterized by increasing stratification and division. Towns grew in importance, notably the two centers associated with Muhammad—Mecca and Medina.

These and other Arabian settlements came under the power of a merchant oligarchy, which also controlled the new money economy. To demystify Islam, we must first demystify its history—which means understanding the significant threat it posed to these commercial and political interests.

At the same time, it is important to notice that religious practices during this time were also becoming more centralized. Smaller tribes abandoned their local shrines and increasingly venerated those favored by larger groups. While household gods and other religious symbols denoting kinship ties of the older society continued to exist until the advent of Islam, there was an increasing tendency for Arabians to worship a particular deity above others. Mecca's Ka`ba housed relics and artifacts of all the relevant deities—more than 300 of them.

Muhammad at Mecca

Muhammad was born about 570 CE into an impoverished branch of the main merchant family in the trading city of Mecca, an important junction of caravan routes along which products of the Arabian Peninsula were carried to the Mediterranean. In terms of kinship and lineage, he was well placed, but he was orphaned at an early age and grew up in difficult economic circumstances.

Muslims praying before the Ka`ba in the city of Mecca.
Credit: Ahmad Faizal Yahya/Getty Images

Many chroniclers have attempted to paint a picture of an unusual, even fantastic childhood, but Muhammad seems to have been, according to authentic accounts, a serious, intelligent, altogether normal young man. From a very early age, he impressed his fellow citizens as an individual of integrity and enjoyed widespread respect and admiration. In his teens, he was nicknamed "the Trustworthy."

Muhammad's personality is inseparable from any discussion of Islam. He is seen by Muslims as the messenger of God to the world. In addition to the Qur'an, his prophetic example, known as the *Sunnah*, also forms part of the central teaching of Islam.

CAREFUL! *Muslims view Muhammad as the "seal of the prophets," in that he both confirmed previous revelations and was last in the series of divinely appointed messengers. Although he is considered a mere mortal in one sense, he is also the religious symbol of God in another sense. Mainstream Islamic dogma defines him as infallible. In mentioning his name in ordinary speech,*

Muslims offer prayer and salute him by saying, silently or audibly, depending on the circumstances, "May God's peace and blessings be upon him." Disrespect toward the Prophet violates both a centuries-old taboo and a deep aspect of Muslim identity. His own personal response to the manifestly disrespectful treatment he encountered in Mecca, however, was one of patience and tolerance.

Biographers record that from an early age, Muhammad showed deep concern for the injustices of his society. The main features of Arab society at the time were the oppression of the poor and the weak, fratricidal tribal wars, gender discrimination, slavery, and commercial exploitation. Muhammad often retired in isolation to a cave called Hira in Mecca in order to reflect and contemplate. On one such occasion, around his fortieth birthday, in the year 610, he had a vision. In that vision, the Archangel Gabriel (Jibreel) appeared and declared, *Proclaim!* This was the first revelation of the Qur'an.

A page from the Qur'an, the Muslim holy scripture. Muslims believe it was revealed by the angel Gabriel to Muhammad in stages over a period of twenty-three years.

Credit: Purestock/Superstock

"Proclaim! [or Read!] in the name of thy Lord and Cherisher,
Who created—
Created man, out of a [mere] clot of congealed blood:
Proclaim! And thy Lord is Most Bountiful—
He Who taught [the use of] the Pen—
Taught man that which he knew not."

—*Qur'an 96 1:5, the first reported revelation. Translation by Yusuf Ali*

This supernatural event—as Muslims regard it—marked the beginning of thirteen difficult years of prophetic mission in Mecca. Muhammad's central message stressed the supremacy of Allah, the only deity worthy of worship, rejecting at the same time the multitude of gods that the majority of people in the Arabian Peninsula worshipped.

KEY TERMS DEMYSTIFIED: Allah

The Arabic word for "God." It appears in pre-Islamic texts (for instance, those of Arabian Christians) as the name of the God of Abraham.

Reaction to Muhammad

Initially, Muhammad was ignored or ridiculed by all but a few followers. As the Prophet's movement and ideas gained a small but significant number of converts, however, there was increasing opposition from Mecca's mercantile aristocracy, whose materialism and greed Muhammad condemned.

The hostility of this opposition eventually led to both economic sanctions and fatal violence against the tiny but growing band of Muslims. It also led to an assassination plot against Muhammad himself. Many representatives of the elite economic interests of Mecca—members of Muhammad's own tribe, the Quraish—set themselves as implacable enemies of the new faith.

The plot to kill Muhammad failed, however, and he led a Hijrah (exodus or immigration) with his family and a few followers in 622 to the town of Yathrib, some 300 miles north of Mecca. This migration formed the turning point in the development of Islam. In subsequent Muslim history, the Hijrah marks the start of the Islamic calendar, signifying the beginning of a new community.

Medina

When the exiled Prophet arrived in Yathrib, or Medina (the City of the Prophet, as it came to be known), conditions there were favorable for the new faith. The existing socioreligious order was riven by internecine strife between the two main tribes. Like Mecca, Medina was undergoing social change. Here, Muhammad increasingly assumed the dual role of spiritual and temporal leader.

Soon after his arrival in Yathrib, it became necessary to defend Muslims from attack. At the same time, Muhammad's primary objective was to spread his message as widely as possible with the greatest degree of success. To do this he employed the longstanding Arab military traditions of raiding and plundering one's enemies, which he infused with the notion of jihad, or moral struggle.

One of his first strategic moves was to strike at the commercial trade routes that supported the Meccan economy. Meccan caravans had to pass Medina on their way to the prosperous markets of Syria. Muhammad's plan was to weaken Mecca so that he might establish Islam there, in what was already the religious capital of Arabia. The journey back to Mecca—a symbolic return to the Ka`ba of Abraham after the Hijrah—would thus be crucial.

Muhammad's Last Years

After several encounters between his forces and the Meccan army, the Prophet marched into Mecca in 630 in a surprise but bloodless takeover of the city. This momentous victory marked the fulfillment of the Prophet's wish to make Mecca the spiritual home of Islam. Within a decade, the outcast of Mecca had united the greater part of Arabia under his authority.

In 632, the last year of his life, Muhammad led the first Islamic pilgrimage to Mecca, where he delivered his historic Farewell Pilgrimage speech. The speech covered a wide range of moral and social issues and enunciated some of the central beliefs in Islam: humanitarianism, egalitarianism, social and economic justice, righteousness, and solidarity. A summary of the principal ideas it contained appears in the following edited version of this famous address:

> O People, lend me an attentive ear, for I know not whether after this year, I shall ever be amongst you again. Therefore listen to what I am saying to you very carefully and take these words to those who could not be present here today.[1]
>
> O People . . . regard the life and property of every Muslim as a sacred trust. Return the goods entrusted to you to their rightful owners. Hurt no one so that no one may hurt you. Remember that you will indeed meet your Lord, and that He will indeed reckon your deeds. Allah has forbidden you to take usury [interest], therefore all interest obligation shall henceforth be waived. Your capital, however, is yours to keep. You will neither inflict nor suffer any inequity. Allah has judged that there shall be no interest and that all the interest due to Abbas ibn 'Abd'al Muttalib [the Prophet's uncle] shall henceforth be waived. . . .
>
> Beware of Satan, for the safety of your religion. He has lost all hope that he will ever be able to lead you astray in big things, so beware of following him in small things.
>
> O People, it is true that you have certain rights with regard to your women, but they also have rights over you. Remember that you have taken them as your wives only under Allah's trust and with His permission. If they abide by your right then to them belongs the right to be fed and clothed in kindness. Do treat your women well and be kind to them for they are your partners and committed helpers. And it is your right that they do not make friends with anyone of whom you do not approve, as well as never to be unchaste. . . . All mankind is from Adam and Eve, an Arab has no superiority over a non-Arab nor a non-Arab has any superiority over an Arab; also a white has no superiority over black nor a black has any superiority over white except by piety and good action. Learn that every Muslim is a brother to every Muslim and that the Muslims constitute one brotherhood. Nothing shall be legitimate to a Muslim which belongs to a fellow Muslim unless it was given freely and willingly. Do not, therefore, do injustice to yourselves.
>
> Remember, one day you will appear before Allah and answer your deeds. So beware, do not stray from the path of righteousness after I am gone.

---

[1] "Farewell Sermon of the Prophet Muhammad (632)." *Oxford Islamic Studies Online.* 04-Feb-2014. http://www.oxfordislamicstudies.com/article/doc/ps-islam-0201.

O People, no prophet or apostle will come after me and no new faith will be born. Reason well, therefore, O People, and understand words which I convey to you. I leave behind me two things, the Qur'an and my example, the Sunnah, and if you follow these you will never go astray.

All those who listen to me shall pass on my words to others and those to others again; and may the last ones understand my words better than those who listen to me directly. Be my witness, O Allah, that I have conveyed your message to your people. – *From the Prophet Muhammad's final sermon*

Muhammad died in 632. His legacy among the global community of Muslims is that of the restorer of the unaltered monotheistic faith of Adam, Noah, Abraham, Moses, Jesus, and other prophets. His legacy among non-Muslims is more complex, but most scholars of history regard him as one of the most important and influential figures of any era. Some—such as the non-Muslim historian Michael Hart—even identify him as the most influential person who ever lived.

Summary

- Islam, a monotheistic faith whose adherents worship the God of Abraham, is regarded by its followers as a continuation of the Eternal Religion preached by all authentic Prophets.

- Muslims regard Muhammad as the final Prophet of God. He preached an unyielding monotheism, rejected polytheism, and emphasized humanitarianism, egalitarianism, social and economic justice, righteousness, and solidarity among Muslims.

- Muhammad lived in Arabia during a time of great social change. He reported a series of divine revelations; his preaching following these revelations won him bitter enemies in the economically and religiously important city of Mecca. After economic privation, persecution, and violence against his followers—and an assassination plot against Muhammad that failed—the Muslims made a Hijrah (emigration) to the city of Medina. There, conditions were favorable to the development of the faith.

- A series of military conflicts against his enemies in Mecca culminated in the bloodless takeover of the City of Mecca by the Muslims. There, in 632, Muhammad led the first Islamic pilgrimage to the city, and delivered his Farewell Pilgrimage sermon.

QUIZ

1. **Near the end of the sixth century CE, Muhammad, the Prophet of Islam, was born in**

   A. Africa.

   B. Arabia.

   C. Jerusalem.

   D. None of the above.

2. **Muslims regard Islam as**

   A. a new and untested religion.

   B. the purification and reconstitution of the unique monotheistic faith that God provided for humankind from the very beginning.

   C. a compendium of all religious movements.

   D. None of the above.

3. **The words *Islam* and *Muslim* both originate from the Arabic root S-L-M, which means roughly**

   A. "to be safe and free."

   B. "to transform."

   C. "to open."

   D. None of the above.

4. **The origins and content of Islam cannot be viewed in isolation from the religious history of**

   A. Taoism and Buddhism.

   B. Hinduism and Shinto.

   C. Judaism and Christianity.

   D. None of the above.

5. **Muslims regard Jews and Christians as**

   A. "People of the Book."

   B. "People of the Ka`ba."

   C. "People of Islam."

   D. None of the above.

6. **The Ka`ba housed**

    A. armaments.

    B. relics and artifacts of all the popular deities of the time—more than 300 of them.

    C. the original holy scriptures from Christianity and Judaism.

    D. None of the above.

7. **The city where the Ka`ba is located is known as**

    A. Jerusalem.

    B. Medina.

    C. Mecca.

    D. None of the above.

8. **Muslims believe that, at the age of 40, Muhammad**

    A. received a revelation from the Archangel Gabriel.

    B. traveled to Jerusalem by miraculous means.

    C. meditated under a palm tree for 40 days.

    D. None of the above.

9. **The city to which the Prophet Muhammad emigrated after an unsuccessful assassination attempt is now known as**

    A. Jerusalem.

    B. Medina.

    C. Mecca.

    D. None of the above.

10. **The Muslim holy scripture is known as**

    A. the Hadiths.

    B. the Farewell Sermon.

    C. the Qur'an.

    D. None of the above.

chapter **14**

Islam: Core Beliefs and Practices

This chapter's topic takes on a peculiar importance in our time. For a faith system that is as widely practiced and as closely related to the other important mono-theistic faiths as Islam, there remains a surprising amount of confusion about what Muslims actually believe and practice. In fact, of all the faith systems for which demystifying might seem to be in order, none appears today to be more in need of demystification to outsiders than Islam.

Why? In this chapter, we will try to answer that question.

CHAPTER OBJECTIVES

In this chapter, you'll learn about:

- What Muslims believe
- Obligations of Islamic life

Extremism

What makes so many non-Muslims distrustful of Islam? We pose the question directly here, and as the first question of this chapter, for three reasons. First, because we live in a time when prejudice against Muslims has become the norm rather than the exception—a troubling development, perhaps, within societies that are supposedly built upon the foundation of religious pluralism. Second, because ignoring this question or minimizing it generally only makes it harder for people to understand Islam's core tenets. (In other words, people may come to believe that information about Islam is being hidden if this question is left unaddressed.) And third, because we believe the answer to this question is not just instructive in terms of demystifying Islam, but essential.

So we begin this chapter by answering the question directly. The factor that makes non-Muslims distrustful of Islam is extremism.

Extremism is defined by the Free Dictionary as follows: "The practice of advocating or resorting to measures well beyond the norm, especially in politics."

The important thing to be said about extremism as it relates to Islam is this: first, last, and always, extremism is forbidden to Muslims. The Prophet once said, "The extremists will perish" and repeated it three times as a stern warning to his followers.

You have already seen, in the previous chapter, that the Prophet Muhammad explicitly instructed his followers to maintain strict obedience to (1) his own example and teachings, especially where he identified red lines not to be crossed and (2) the guidance of the Qur'an. By the way, those are the two key criteria when it comes to determining ethical practice in any and all areas of a Muslim's life: the example and teachings of the Prophet, on the one hand, and the Qur'an on the other. Far from being separate entities, they are regarded as elements of a unified whole. A classic metaphor compares the faith of the believer to a bird in flight: one wing is the Sunnah of the Prophet, and the other wing is the Qur'an. The bird needs both in order to fly. The metaphor of two wings used is faith and knowledge or faith and practice.

So let's look now at what both of these "wings" offer to the faithful on the question of extremism. Any Muslim who advocates political measures that violate the ethical red lines identified by the Prophet is engaged in *sin*.

It is important to point out here that the Prophet's norm on issues such as war, peace, and education is clear. Countless scholars have attested to these norms over many centuries. This norm bears very deep scrutiny by Muslim and non-Muslim alike. So, for instance, advocating suicide or participating in it, or targeting civilians as though they were combatants, or preventing the education of women and girls—these are all behaviors that fall well beyond the norm. These behaviors cannot possibly be justified by the teachings, behavior, or example of the Prophet. These are all forbidden acts. These acts are in violation of both the teachings of the Sunnah and the Qur'an.

The second wing, of course, is the Qur'an, the holy text of Islam. Here is what the Qur'an has to say on the topic of extremism:

> Thus, have We made of you an Ummah (community) justly balanced (literally, "a middle nation"), that ye might be witnesses over the nations, and the Apostle a witness over yourselves. (2:143)

The Qur'an thus envisions a middle community of Muslims, a moderate community of Muslims. Does the Qur'an countenance the random killing of "infidels"? You might think so, to hear extremists (Muslim and non-Muslim alike) who take the verses out of context and then quote a few carefully selected syllables at a time. What you will find when you read the relevant selections closely, however, is that Muslims are permitted to defend themselves when attacked. They must engage in battle only with those who eject them from their homes and prohibit them from practicing their religion. They must cease conflict when the other side sues for peace.

> But if the enemy inclines toward peace, do thou (also) incline towards peace, and trust in Allah: for He is One that heareth and knoweth (all things). (Qur'an 8:61)

Please see the figure on page 167 in Chapter 13, which refers to the Arabic calligraphy in the Qur'an.

> It may be that Allah will grant love [and friendship] between you and those whom ye (now) hold as enemies. For Allah has power [over all things], and Allah is Oft-Forgiving, Most Merciful. God does not forbid you, with regard to those who fight you not for [your] faith nor drive you out of your homes, from dealing kindly and justly with them: for Allah loves those who are just. (Qur'an 60:7-8)

These, then, are the facts of what Islam teaches about extremism. Regardless of any individual's intention or justification, these are the guidelines, binding upon all Muslims, that appear in the Sunnah and the Qur'an.

A few final observations on extremism are, perhaps, in order here.

Extremism can pervert any faith, not just the Islamic faith. Many in the United States and elsewhere operate today under widespread distrust of Muslims, and of Islam, because of the actions of a tiny minority of well-publicized extremists. These people are dangerous, of course, and it is natural that there should be emotional reactions to their crimes. Yet we may pass too quickly over the question of whether *most* terrorist attacks are perpetrated by Muslims (they are not, according to both the FBI and the European Union; see http://bit.ly/1aZrLgK). Similarly, we may pass too quickly over the question of whether Muslims themselves are safe from random terror attacks against civilians (they are not; several dozen Muslims died in the 9/11 attacks, and Muslims remain among the most likely target of extremist hate crimes in the United States and also make up the largest number of victims of extremist violence abroad).

We may pass too quickly over another question, too. It is this: Why does a demented pair of Muslim bombers in Boston who kill three people perpetuate a new round of global fear and mistrust about the true intentions of Islam—while a demented Christian gunman in Norway who kills 77 people does not raise similar questions about the true intentions of Christianity? Of course, none of these criminals have anything authoritative to say concerning religion. The criminally insane are not reliable sources of spiritual guidance, in Islam or any other tradition.

CAREFUL! *There are two (main) denominations within Islam, not to be confused with one another. Sunni Muslims, the majority group, make up between 75 and 90 percent of the global body of believers; Shia Muslims constitute between 10 and 20 percent of the total. Shia Muslims form majorities in countries such as Iran and Iraq. Both groups accept the Qur'an as the unerring, literal word of God, but there are important differences between the two. The differences— cultural, historical, and scholarly—are stark and significant, and extend deep into Islamic history. A core disagreement between the two denominations concerns the nephew of the Prophet, Ali, regarded by Shia Muslims as the divinely appointed successor of the Prophet Muhammad and the first rightful Imam (leader) of the faithful. Sunni Muslims accept Ali as an exemplary role model and a rightly guided Caliph (successor), but reject the notion that he was designated by Muhammad before his death as the rightful next leader of the Muslims.*

What Do Muslims Believe?

There are six articles of Islamic faith.

1. **Belief in God (Allah).** There is one and only one worthy of all worship—and the accompanying belief that Muhammad is his messenger. The Arabic word *Allah* simply means "the one God" and predates Muhammad. The formal name for Islam's uncompromising doctrine on the unity of the Creator is *Tawhid*, and it is not to be mistaken for a belief that Muhammad the Prophet of Islam is divine. This supposition that Muslims worship Muhammad is a common mistake, one that only distances outsiders from the faith's key article of belief. (For a century or more, the unfortunate label *Mohammadanism* persisted in Europe, and it served only to divide, never to illuminate.) The concept of monotheism in Islam is the most fundamental precept of this deen, or way of life. It holds the Divine to be one (wāḥid) and unique (aḥad), a unified and absolute truth that transcends and is independent of the entire creation. This Creator is not to be confused with any aspect of the creation. It is not a local, tribal, or parochial entity, but rather an absolute, beyond all limited notions and opposites.

2. **Belief in the angels.** Islam shares with the mainstream schools of Judaism and Christianity an insistence on the reality of these heavenly beings, which are mentioned repeatedly in the Qur'an. Muslims regard angels as differing from human beings and jinn (spiritual creatures) in their lack of free will. Angels must do what Allah orders them to do.

3. **Belief in the Books sent by God (including the Qur'an).** Among the sacred books acknowledged in the Qur'an as having been sent down by Allah are the Psalms (Zaboor), the Torah (Taurat), and the Gospel (Injeel). It is important to note, however, that Muslims believe in these books as they were delivered, in their original divine form, and that they regard current Jewish and Christian scriptures as having been adulterated over time.

4. **Belief in all the Prophets and Messengers sent by God.** Muslims hold that Muhammad was the last in a long line of Prophets who uncompromisingly preached the Oneness of Allah and the necessity of obedience to Him. Although they worship no Prophet, they acknowledge a shared faith with, and the authority of, all the Prophets who preceded Muhammad. Among those identified by name in the Qur'an are Noah (Nuh), Abraham (Ibrahim), Moses (Musa), and Jesus (Isa). It often comes as a surprise to non-Muslims to learn the degree to

which the text of the Qur'an focuses on the prophetic missions of these figures. To provide some sense of the importance of these figures, we note that Moses (Musa) is the human being most often mentioned by name in the Qur'an; his name appears in the text 136 times. Muhammad, by contrast, is mentioned 4 times.

5. **Belief in the day of judgment and in the resurrection.** Muslims believe in Allah's final assessment of humankind, in a Day of Resurrection (*Qiyamah*) that incorporates the extinction of all life, its restoration, and its judgment. The theme of an impending judgment of humanity is a repeated one within the Qur'an.

6. **Belief in the measure of good and evil.** *Qadr*, the Arabic word generally translated as "destiny," actually suggests the measuring out of some commodity or the establishment of a limit that connects to it. Many scholarly disputes over the precise meaning of this term have led to division, confusion, and disagreement among Muslims concerning this core belief. Rather than add to that confusion, we point out that the early Muslims defined the term in question by pointing out that whatever hits you was never going to miss you, and whatever misses you was never going to hit you.

Obligations of Islamic Life

Islam has many obligations, and five classic "pillars" of faith. These are five basic acts in Islam, considered obligatory by believers and observed as the foundation of Muslim life. They are not mentioned in the Qur'an but are summarized in a famous tradition relating a visit by the Angel Gabriel to the Prophet Muhammad.

These obligations are regarded as mandatory by all Muslims (although Sunni and Shia believers use different terms to describe them). They are central practices of Islamic life.

- **Shahada (belief).** The belief or confession of faith. The Arabic word carries the connotation of "bearing witness" in a public sense. Muslims bear witness that there is no God but God, and that Muhammad is His messenger.
- **Salat (formal prayer).** The practice of formal prayer in Islam, involving standing, bowing, and prostration in prescribed routines. It is mandatory, five times

SPIRITUALLY SPEAKING

"It is necessary for man to know that there is one God who has no Companion, who neither begets nor is begotten, who has no equal and has accepted none as His son . . . who has no co-ruler of the universe with Him. . . . He is the director of the heavens and of the earth and of all things on land and water. . . . He speaks but not with organs like those of human beings. Only those attributes should be ascribed to Him which He has Himself ascribed or those which His Prophets have ascribed to Him . . . the word of God is not created. He has spoken through [Archangel] Gabriel and has revealed it to his Prophet [Muhammad]. . . . One should know that faith is speech, action and thought: speech with the tongue, action with the body and limbs. Faith may become greater and smaller—greater by obedience and smaller by sin. Faith has various stages and divisions. The highest expression of faith is the confession, 'There is no God but Allah,' and the lowest expression of faith is to remove an obstacle from a public road. . . . One must love all the Companions of the Prophet. They are the best of human beings after the Prophet. . . . We should invoke God's mercy for all the Companions. . . . Neglect of prayer is of unbelief, who so neglects it is an unbeliever and remains so until he repents and prays. . . . Such are the doctrines of the people who follow the Tradition (Sunna) and subscribe to the way of the Community."

—*Caliph al-Qadir, Confession of Faith, AD 1041*

a day, with a few exceptions (such as for menstruating women, who are excused from it, and for travelers, who may combine certain prayers). Minor differences in the performance of the prayer are acknowledged between the Shia and Sunni denominations, and between various jurisprudences within each denomination. Salat always involves recitation of the Qur'an, sometimes silently and sometimes chanted aloud. The performance of the mandatory daily prayers is seen as the dividing line between belief and disbelief. A ritual ablution (wudu) must be in place in order for any prayer to be valid. In addition to the formal daily prayers, there are additional "traditional" (Sunnah) prayers that are seen as earning merit for the Muslim who performs them; consciously omitting these prayers, however, is not regarded as sinful. Other optional (nafl) prayers may be performed at any time, and for any reason, and are seen as bestowing blessings on those who make them.

- **Sawm Ramadan (fasting during the month of Ramadan).** Abstaining from food, drink, and sexual intercourse is mandatory for all Muslims during the holy month of Ramadan, although exceptions to the fasting are made for the ill, for menstruating and pregnant women, and for travelers. Muslims are encouraged to be generous in this month and give optional charity over and above the mandatory charity of zakat. A common misconception about the monthlong Ramadan fast is the notion that it must be maintained for 24 hours a day. In fact, it is only required during daylight hours. (Extremes of asceticism are forbidden in Islam.)

- **Zakat (alms or charitable giving).** This is a preset, mandatory tax upon wealth that is seen as purifying one's wealth. Optional charity (sadaqa) falls under a different category.

- **Hajj (the pilgrimage to Mecca).** This, too, is mandatory; it is to be undertaken at least once in a lifetime by each and every Muslim. Those who live far away from Mecca and cannot afford the journey are excused, but encouraged to find means and to make a prayerful commitment to complete the journey in the future. The hajj is primarily a way to memorialize the trials and tribulations of the Prophet Abraham, his slave wife Hagar, and her son, Ishmael. God gave Abraham instructions to sacrifice his son, who was miraculously replaced by a ram, and Ishmael was saved. Abraham and Ishmael built a house of worship called the Ka`ba, a cubic room, which is the focal point of Muslims in their daily prayers and annual pilgrimage.

There are other obligations in Islam, all undertaken as worship. Among them is the obligation to dress modestly (and in the case of the observant female, to cover the hair and neck), to take part in the two communal holidays Eid al-Fitr and Eid al-Adha, and to be sure one's children are taught the Qur'an. In a broader sense, all Muslims are obliged to encounter the Qur'an and learn from it on a daily basis. The Prophet Muhammad encouraged both men and women to learn and expand their educational horizons.

KEY TERMS DEMYSTIFIED: Sharia

Anybody studying Islam or who has contact with Muslims inevitably encounters this term. Wrongly translated as Islamic law, **Sharia** is ethics. Literally. *Sharia* means "a path," and technically it means "that which is revealed." Muslim scholars try to make sense of God's revelation and the Prophet Muhammad's teachings using reason and other modes of interpretation. Ethics deal with the duties owed to God and the reciprocal claims and duties between humans. So Muslim ethics rely on a commitment to God, an obligation to reason, and the need to obtain the greatest good. Sometimes Muslims also use the term *fiqh*, meaning "understanding," interchangeably with *Sharia*.

There are a number of ancient schools of interpretation of Muslim ethical and legal practices that continue to this very day. All ritual practices and social and ethical practices are filtered through the teachings of Sharia. Sharia is sometimes part of the country's public policy as in Iran or Saudi Arabia, or at times only part of Sharia is applied in matters of family law. Where Muslims are in a minority, Sharia is part of their private practice, in the same way that Halacha is part of Jewish private practice in places outside of the modern state of Israel.

SPIRITUALLY SPEAKING

"Learning only unveils herself to one who wholeheartedly gives himself up to her; who approaches her with an unclouded mind and clear insight; who seeks God's help and focuses an undivided attention upon learning. ... He should discriminate between the doubtful and certain, between genuine and spurious and should always stand firm by the clear light of reason."

—*Mutahhar bin Abdullah, tenth century*

If pressed to identify one element of Islamic practice that all Muslims would agree upon, that distinguishes this faith from other belief systems, and that connects intimately to the theme of learning as an ongoing obligation, we would cite the centrality of the Qur'an. This revelation is pervasive to the life of a Muslim and is, ultimately, the best exponent of Islam. It is the ultimate tool for the demystification of what this belief system is all about.

Verse of the Light

Allah is the Light of the heavens and the earth.

The Parable of His Light is as if there were a Niche and within it a Lamp,

The Lamp enclosed in Glass: the glass: as it were a brilliant star,

Lit from a blessed Tree, an Olive, neither of the east nor of the west, whose oil is well-nigh luminous, though fire scarce touched it.

Light upon Light! Allah doth guide whom He will to His Light.

Allah doth set forth Parables for men: and Allah doth know all things.

—*Qur'an 24:35, translated by Abdullah Yusuf Ali*

Sufism: Islam's Mystical Expression

In response to the perceived worldliness and secularism of the Umayyad Caliphate, which assumed political control over the expanding Islamic empire in the late seventh century, a mystical movement emerged. This movement emphasized intense meditative and esoteric practices, and it took quite literally the famous injunction attributed to the Prophet Muhammad regarding the spiritual goal of ihsan: "To worship Allah as though you are seeing Him, and while you see Him not, yet truly He sees you."

KEY TERMS DEMYSTIFIED: Mysticism

Mystical movements exist in all major religious systems. Mysticism strives for the direct experience of the divine and can be distinguished from traditional religious practice by its emphasis on the personal attainment of distinctive, transcendent states of consciousness, typically through prayer, meditation, or remembrance.

The movement took the name *tasawwuf*, which literally means "to dress in wool." This is a reference to the ascetic garments of the original members of the school. In English-speaking countries, this expression of Islam is known as Sufism, and its adherents are known as Sufis.

KEY TERMS DEMYSTIFIED: Sufis

Followers of the Islamic mystic tradition. There are many schools of Sufism, each with a unique lineage. All these schools trace their beliefs, practices, and spiritual commitment to the teachings and example of the Prophet Muhammad, emphasizing in particular his teachings concerning *ihsan*. This is a word without any exact English counterpart. It has been variously translated as "purity," "sincerity," "refining," or "perfection." Its broader meaning addresses perfection of worship through securing the absence of any other element in one's life than the desire to please and obey the Creator.

The Sufi discourse seeks to combine the Sharia and the spiritual path. It often focuses on the literal meaning of things as the entry point to their inner meaning, which tends toward allegory and symbolism. For instance, some Sufis provide as an illustration the symbol of a geometric circle. From the center, any number of radii connect with the outer border—the circumference of the circle. That circumference represents the Sharia, the ethical principles that define and guide the Muslim community. Each radius within the circle, however, symbolizes a valid spiritual path that emanates from the center. This center, in turn, represents Truth, also known as Haqiqa. It is this center, Sufis maintain, that is the source of both the Sharia and the personal spiritual experience.

Sufis consider themselves proponents of Islam in its authentic, original form. In both ancient and contemporary times, they have drawn their share of skepticism and opposition from self-described proponents of orthodox Islam. According to some of its critics, Sufism has been too heavily influenced by elements of various other faiths. Its more earnest practitioners deny these claims, but a careful evaluation suggests that, while Sufism was initially located within the prophetic and Quranic framework, many practices adopted later share features of mysticism found in other, non-Islamic traditions.

Islam in a Box	
Divinity	Allah. The concept of God in Islam is entirely monotheistic.
Afterlife	Questioning in the grave, Day of Judgment, then Jannah (heaven) or Jahanam (hell).
Purpose of Human Life	Worship and obedience to Allah. To live as if this life is temporary and the afterlife is permanent. Obedience to Allah in any action is worship.
Distinctive Practices and Beliefs	The belief in Tawhid (worship of one God who has no children, associates, or partners). Physical ritual prayers five times a day. A month of fasting during Ramadan. Pilgrimage to Mecca, Saudi Arabia, at least once in one's lifetime if one can afford it. Payment of a poor-tax. Muslims must dress modestly; they are forbidden alcohol and pork; smoking tobacco is discouraged since it is damaging to health.
Outsiders Often Distracted by	The hijab or niqab worn by Muslim women. The hijab is a head covering, while the niqab covers the face. The obligation in Islam is modesty. Many outsiders believe these garments reflect an oppression of women. Observant Muslim women wear a variety of apparels to express their modesty in dress. These range from no head covering to hijab and niqab or other forms of cultural dress. Those who wear hijab often do so by choice or as part of a public culture. In places like Saudi Arabia and Iran, women are required to wear either the niqab or hijab in public. In countries like Pakistan, Egypt, or Tunisia, women choose to wear modest dress of differing types.

Summary

- Islam unambiguously prohibits extremism.

- The six articles of Islamic faith are belief in God (Allah); belief in the Angels; belief in the Books sent by God (including the Qur'an); belief in all the Prophets and Messengers sent by God; belief in the Day of Judgment and in the Resurrection; belief in the Measure of Good and Evil.

- There are many mandatory practices in Islam. Five famous "pillars" of the faith are shahada (belief or confession of faith), salat (worship in the form of prayer), sawm Ramadan (fasting during the month of Ramadan), zakat (alms or charitable giving), and hajj (the pilgrimage to Mecca).

- Sharia (often mistranslated as "Islamic Law") is ethics that deal with the duties owed to God and the reciprocal claims and duties between humans. Muslim ethics rely on a commitment to God, an obligation to reason, and the need to obtain the greatest good. All ritual practices and social and ethical practices are filtered through the teachings of Sharia.

QUIZ

1. **Islam demands obedience to**
   A. the Sunnah of the prophet Muhammad.
   B. the Qur'an.
   C. both the Sunnah of the prophet Muhammad and the Qur'an.
   D. None of the above.

2. **Shia Muslims believe**
   A. the Qur'an has been modified, and its original text is unknown.
   B. the Sunnah of the Prophet Muhammad is irrelevant.
   C. the Prophet Muhammad's nephew Ali was the divinely appointed successor of the Prophet.
   D. None of the above.

3. **Sunni Muslims believe**
   A. the Qur'an has been modified, and its original text is unknown.
   B. the Sunnah of the Prophet Muhammad is irrelevant.
   C. the prophet Muhammad's nephew Ali was the divinely appointed successor of the Prophet.
   D. None of the above.

4. **The so-called five pillars of Islam include**
   A. prayer (salat).
   B. fasting (sawm).
   C. paying a religious tax (zakat).
   D. All of the above.

5. **Sharia is best understood as**
   A. Islamic ethics.
   B. Islamic law.
   C. Islamic interfaith outreach.
   D. None of the above.

6. **Salat (formal Islamic prayer) always involves**
   A. recitation of the Christian New Testament.
   B. recitation of the Hebrew scriptures.
   C. recitation of the Qur'an.
   D. None of the above.

7. **In Islam, intentional neglect of mandatory prayers is considered**
   A. disbelief.
   B. a minor matter.
   C. an issue best resolved by the individual's family.
   D. None of the above.

8. **Muslims believe in**
   A. angels.
   B. the Books sent by God (including the Qur'an).
   C. all the Prophets and Messengers sent by God.
   D. All of the above.

9. **Islam requires that**
   A. both men and women dress modestly.
   B. only women dress modestly.
   C. each individual dress according to his or her own tastes, or even go nude if he or she so chooses.
   D. None of the above.

10. **True or false: Women are prohibited from pursuing higher education in Islam.**

PART TWO TEST

In this part of the book, you will test your mastery of monotheistic religious traditions as you prepare for the Final Exam at the end of the book. You will also identify which, if any, of the three monotheistic religious traditions you've just studied should be reviewed a little more closely before you tackle that test.

Schedule a half hour to an hour of uninterrupted time to see just how well you have mastered the content presented in Chapters 9 through 14. This preliminary test will tell you where you are strongest—and where you still need to review content relating to Judaism, Christianity, and Islam.

1. **Judaism is a _____ belief system.**
   A. polytheistic
   B. pantheistic
   C. monotheistic
   D. nihilistic

2. **Tanakh is a**
   A. distinctive Hebrew term for Judaism's core religious scriptures, beginning with the book of Genesis and ending with the book of Chronicles.
   B. covering used during a Jewish wedding.
   C. rite of conversion in Judaism.
   D. None of the above.

3. **The Torah is**
   A. the last five books of the Hebrew Scriptures.
   B. the first five books of the Hebrew Scriptures.
   C. the first five commentaries of the Talmud.
   D. None of the above.

4. **True or false:** *Orthodoxy* **means "correctness in action, rather than belief."**

5. **The Goden Rule**
   A. maintains that what one would wish to experience personally should guide the behavior one employs in interactions with others.
   B. establishes gold as a medium of exchange.
   C. is unique to Judaism.
   D. None of the above.

6. **A synagogue is**

   A. a Jewish scripture.

   B. a Jewish house of prayer.

   C. a Jewish community leader.

   D. None of the above.

7. **Orthodox Jews**

   A. accept the entire Torah as the definitive guide for modern life.

   B. hold that traditional Jewish Law is subject to critical evaluation and are more likely to interpret that law as a body of broad guidelines rather than as a set of binding restrictions on Jewish behavior.

   C. aim to conserve certain traditional elements of Judaism while also allowing for modernization.

   D. None of the above.

8. **Reform Jews**

   A. accept the entire Torah as the definitive guide for modern life.

   B. hold that traditional Jewish Law is subject to critical evaluation and are more likely to interpret that law as a body of broad guidelines rather than as a set of binding restrictions on Jewish behavior.

   C. aim to conserve certain traditional elements of Judaism while also allowing for modernization.

   D. None of the above.

9. **Conservative Jews**

   A. accept the entire Torah as the definitive guide for modern life.

   B. hold that traditional Jewish Law is subject to critical evaluation, and are more likely to interpret that law as a body of broad guidelines rather than as a set of binding restrictions on Jewish behavior.

   C. aim to conserve certain traditional elements of Judaism while also allowing for modernization.

   D. None of the above.

10. **A rabbi**

   A. is the same as a Jewish priest.

   B. is a teacher who has been adequately educated in Jewish law and tradition; this education allows the rabbi to teach and advise the community according to Jewish law.

   C. is the only person who can lead Jewish prayer services.

   D. None of the above.

11. *Apostle* is

    A. a Greek word meaning "emissary."
    B. a term that may be taken to mean one of the original Jewish followers of Jesus commissioned to spread the good news of his ministry.
    C. a term that may also be used to include later converts such as Paul of Tarsus, the "apostle to the Gentiles."
    D. All of the above.

12. **The most successful Christian missionary of the first-century world, founded Christian churches in Asia Minor and Europe, and skillfully used his status as a Jew and a citizen of the Roman Empire to support his ministry. His name was**

    A. Paul.
    B. Peter.
    C. John.
    D. Jude.

13. **The Nicene Creed**

    A. was revoked in Constantinople and is no longer observed by contemporary Christians.
    B. is a statement of faith that established the formal Trinitarian doctrine of Christianity, which regards God the Father, God the Son, and God the Holy Spirit as divine.
    C. was the cause of the Great Schism of 1054.
    D. None of the above.

14. **The Protestant Reformation was led by figures such as**

    A. Pope John Paul II.
    B. Martin Luther.
    C. Giordano Bruno.
    D. All of the above.

15. **The Trinity**

    A. was rejected by almost all European Protestants in the sixteenth century.
    B. expresses the scriptural unity of Judaism, Christianity, and Islam.
    C. is an important doctrine of mainstream Christianity identifying "one God in three persons"—God the Father, God the Son, and God the Holy Spirit.
    D. None of the above.

16. **Lent is**

    A. a forty-day period preceding Easter that emphasizes self-examination and self-denial.

    B. the same holiday as Mardi Gras.

    C. the holiday that marks the failure of the Protestant Reformation.

    D. None of the above.

17. **Easter is**

    A. always observed on the same calendar date each year.

    B. a celebration of the birth of Jesus to the Virgin Mary.

    C. a holiday that celebrates the resurrection of Jesus.

    D. All of the above.

18. **Pentecost is**

    A. celebrated forty days after Easter.

    B. celebrated twenty days after Easter.

    C. celebrated ten days after Easter.

    D. None of the above.

19. **Advent is celebrated**

    A. in the month before Christmas.

    B. in the month after Christmas.

    C. on Christmas Day.

    D. None of the above.

20. **Jesus is regarded by mainstream Christians as**

    A. the only begotten Son of God.

    B. an Islamic prophet.

    C. the Jewish patriarch Abraham, reborn.

    D. None of the above.

21. **The Islamic prophet Muhammad was**

    A. born in 570.

    B. born in 632.

    C. born in 667.

    D. None of the above.

22. **The Qur'an is**

    A. the same thing as the Sunnah.

    B. the holy text of Islam.

    C. a compilation of ninth-century Buddhist traditions.

    D. None of the above.

23. **Salat is**

    A. prayer.

    B. fasting.

    C. almsgiving.

    D. pilgrimage.

24. **Zakat is**

    A. prayer.

    B. fasting.

    C. almsgiving.

    D. pilgrimage.

25. **Sawm Ramadan is**

    A. prayer.

    B. fasting.

    C. almsgiving.

    D. pilgrimage.

26. **Hajj is**

    A. prayer.

    B. fasting.

    C. almsgiving.

    D. pilgrimage.

27. **Shahada is**

    A. the belief or confession of faith.

    B. the name of an Islamic angel.

    C. the name of the Prophet Muhammad's first wife.

    D. None of the above.

28. **Ali is regarded as the first legitimate Caliph, or successor to the Prophet Muhammad, by**
    A. Sunni Muslims.
    B. Shia Muslims.
    C. both Sunni and Shia Muslims.
    D. None of the above.

29. **True or false:** *Allah* **is the Arabic word for God.**

30. **The word** *Islam* **comes from the same Arabic root as the word**
    A. *Muslim.*
    B. *Qur'an.*
    C. *Hadith.*
    D. None of the above.

Part Three

Dissenting Voices

The rise of new faith systems in response to existing religious traditions is not an exclusively modern phenomenon, but it certainly seems to have picked up speed and intensity.

In the period leading up to the era in which we live, an increasingly loud chorus of dissenting religious voices made itself heard. In this part of the book, you learn about some of the most significant traditions to stake their claim in realms beyond that of the ancient world and the "big three" monotheistic systems.

chapter **15**

Sikhism: History and Context

Sikhism is a monotheistic faith system founded during the fifteenth century in the Punjab region of the Indian subcontinent. With roughly 30 million practitioners, it is the world's fifth-largest religion. Its adherents are now found in many parts of the world beyond the Punjab.

CHAPTER OBJECTIVES

In this chapter, you'll learn about:

- How Sikhism was founded
- Who Guru Nanak was
- Other Gurus of Sikhism
- How the history of the Punjab intersects with Sikhism

Sikhism has a clear point of origin and connects to a single founder whose historical existence is undisputed. Let's begin by looking at him.

Guru Nanak and the Founding of Sikhism

The founder of Sikhism was born to a Hindu family in what is now the Pakistani Punjab in April 1469. His name was Nanak. As a young boy, he was intensely interested in the study of religion.

CAREFUL! *The English name of this religion is Sikhism; its followers are known as Sikhs. They, however, refer to their faith as* Sikhi. *The root word* Sikh *means "student" or "disciple."*

Tradition tells us Nanak began asking questions about the nature of the Divine at the age of five, and that at the age of seven he astonished his teachers by analyzing the monotheistic implications of the first letter of the alphabet. (That letter, analogous to the English *A*, is formed by a single downstroke in Persian and Arabic, common languages in the region. Thus the first letter of the alphabet strongly resembles the numeral "one.")

The boy is known to have refused to wear Hindu sacred garments, being unwilling to trust in the divine protection of a physical object and preferring an inward faith. Throughout his life and from an early age, his older sister, Bibi Nanki, recognized Nanak's special understanding of religion, and she is considered his first follower and one of the most important. Her importance in the life of Guru Nanak set a precedent for gender equality in Sikhism that would eventually become a central feature of the religion.

After Nanak married and had two children, Nanki's husband helped Nanak acquire a job at a government granary in Sultanpur. Nanak meditated each day by a river before work, and one of these meditations served as the backdrop for his revelations. Nanak, then around thirty, was gone for three days during this meditation, and when he returned, his first words were reportedly "There is no Hindu, there is no Muslim."

From this point forward, he preached the core message of the faith that would eventually transform the region. He promoted an accessible set of monotheistic teachings that relentlessly emphasized tolerance and service.

At the time of the faith's emergence, the dominant religions on the subcontinent were Hinduism and Islam. Sikhism's founding figure, Guru Nanak, both borrowed from and set his religious practice apart from these two faith systems. He preached a distinctive faith that was very closely tied to the peoples and culture of the Punjab, and the religion quickly carved out an enduring niche for itself in the region.

KEY TERMS DEMYSTIFIED: Guru

"Enlightened leader."

Nanak undertook a series of five grand missionary journeys, called *Udasis*, in order to spread his message. The exact destinations of the journeys are a matter of controversy, but traditions hold that the first four Udasis went in each of the cardinal directions, East, South, North, and West, and ranged throughout India, Pakistan, Tibet, and the Arabian countries. The fifth Udasis was a journey around his home region of the Punjab. Throughout all of these journeys, Nanak was accompanied by a Muslim minstrel from his home village named Bhai Mardana, who became an important figure in Sikh religion and scriptures, being traditionally represented as a doubting figure to whom the Guru would explain and clarify his message.

SPIRITUALLY SPEAKING

"Even Kings and emperors with heaps of wealth and vast dominion cannot compare with an ant filled with the love of God."

—*Guru Nanak*

The Udasis served both to spread the Guru's message and to refine it, as he observed the world and the people around him. Two constant themes were worship of the Word of God (Naam Japna) and the importance of following awakened individuals (Gurmukh) rather than the state of self-absorbed will (Manmukh) that leads to frustration and danger.

After his journeys were concluded, Guru Nanak returned to the Punjab to the town of Kartarpur, where he continued to teach and worked in fields to earn his living, helping to provide free food to all who asked for it.

After Nanak

Before his death, Guru Nanak appointed one of his most devoted followers, Bhai Lehna, as the new Guru. (Interestingly, he passed over both of his own sons.) Upon Nanak's death at the age of seventy, Lehna took the name Guru Angad.

Guru Angad had also been raised Hindu, and had first heard Nanak's teaching after taking a detour from a Hindu pilgrimage. Angad was a hugely important Guru, creating the Gurmukhi alphabet, which Sikh scriptures would be written in by modifying Punjabi script, and writing sixty-three couplets that eventually would be incorporated in the formal Sikh scripture.

Guru Angad also created schools to improve literacy and education, and continued to strengthen both the core message and the organizational structure of Sikhism, establishing it as a long-lasting religious movement. He followed Nanak's example and identified his own successor, Sri Amar Das, before his own death at age forty-eight in 1552.

Guru Amar Das was Guru Angad's elder, being seventy years old when he became the Guru, and oversaw the religion's expansion. He emphasized the equality of women and the importance of Langar, the ceremonial sharing of free food among people of all social status. He appointed his son-in-law Jetha Ram Das as the fourth Guru before his death in 1574.

Guru Ram Das authored many important Sikh verses, and formalized the structure of Sikhism, including many of the daily rituals. He died in 1581 and appointed his youngest son, Guru Arjan, to be the next Guru.

A New Dynamic

Up to this point, the followers of the various Gurus had not been subject to any sort of official persecution from the reigning Muslim Mughal Empire. To the contrary, they had often been on cordial terms with the ruling authorities. However, during the period of Guru Arjan's teachings, this changed.

Guru Arjan's continued expansion of the religion included agricultural projects for lower-class farmers and the composition of more than 2,000 hymns that would become part of Sikh scripture. He oversaw the building of an important Sikh gurdwara in the city of Aritsar, which would become known as the Golden Temple. Taken together, all of these changes translated to a much higher profile for Sikhs within the Muslim-controlled Punjab. That led to problems.

KEY TERMS DEMYSTIFIED: Gurdwara

A Sikh house of worship. The name means "gateway to the Guru." The structure is easily recognizable, thanks to tall flagpoles flying the Sikh flag. People from all faiths are welcome within a gurdwara. Free food served there in very large amounts serves as a kind of social magnet, but not as a tool for proselytizing; practitioners do not generally encourage outsiders to join their faith. (Conversions to Sikhism are comparatively rare, but are permitted.)

In 1605 a new Mughal emperor, Jahangir, came to power. Jahangir viewed the expansion of the Sikh religion as a threat to both the state and Islam. He ordered Guru Arjan to remove all references to established Hindu or Islamic ideas from his scriptures. This Guru Arjan refused to do. In response, Jahangir had Guru Arjan tortured and executed in 1606, making Arjan the first Sikh martyr.

The Later Gurus, the Khalsa, and the *Guru Granth Sahib*

Following Guru Arjan's death, Har Gobind became the sixth Sikh Guru. He began to militarize the Sikhs so they could defend themselves from the Mughals. It was at this point that the Gurus became both spiritual and military leaders of the Sikhs. Har Gobind initiated the practice of carrying two swords—the first spiritual, the second temporal—and led the Sikhs during a troubled period that included both periods of calm and periods of intense persecutions. His three successors as Guru—Har Rai, Har Krishan, and Tegh Bahadur—eventually yielded to the tenth Guru of Sikhism, Guru Gobind Singh.

Gobind Singh, a towering figure in the history of the Punjab, established the Khalsa Panth—a now-legendary Sikh army—to do battle against the Mughal regime. His goal was not merely victory over the Mughals (which was achieved after his death) but the creation of a Sikh community that would never again be unable to defend itself. Before dying in 1708 at the hands of the Muslims, he also issued a vitally important decree that altered the course of his faith's history: He identified the scripture of Guru Arjan Dev, known as the Adi Granth Sahib, as the eleventh and final Guru of Sikhism. There would be no human successor to the tenth Guru.

A period of intense Sikh militancy directed against Muslim rule followed the death of Gobind Singh. Eventually, the Mughals fell, although the Sikhs were not their only adversaries.

What began in the Punjab five centuries ago with Guru Nanak's declaration that "There is no Hindu, there is no Muslim" ended up decisively separating the religion from both Islam and Hinduism. This is not surprising, given the faith's core principles, which resemble but are profoundly at odds with those of both Hinduism and Islam. We will look more closely at those beliefs in the next chapter.

SPIRITUALLY SPEAKING

"While you are alive, conquer death, and you shall have no regrets in the end."

—*Guru Granth Sahib*

Sikhism Timeline

The precepts, teachings, and principles of Sikhism are deeply interwoven with the history of the Punjab region. A timeline of the faith shows just how closely the history of Sikhism and the history of the region connect.

- **1469**   Guru Nanak, the founder of Sikhism and first Guru, is born.

- **1526**   Muslims conquer northern India and found the Mughal Empire.

- **1606**   Guru Arjan is tortured and executed by the Mughals, becoming the first Sikh martyr.

- **1675**   Guru Gobind Singh becomes the tenth (and final human) Guru of Sikhism. He establishes the powerful military/religious institution known as the Khalsa and identifies Sikhism's scripture as its perpetual eleventh Guru.

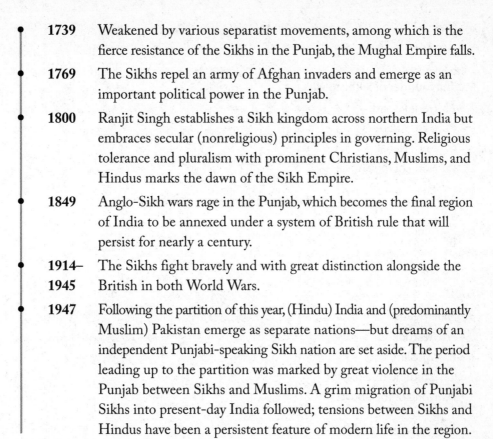

1739 Weakened by various separatist movements, among which is the fierce resistance of the Sikhs in the Punjab, the Mughal Empire falls.

1769 The Sikhs repel an army of Afghan invaders and emerge as an important political power in the Punjab.

1800 Ranjit Singh establishes a Sikh kingdom across northern India but embraces secular (nonreligious) principles in governing. Religious tolerance and pluralism with prominent Christians, Muslims, and Hindus marks the dawn of the Sikh Empire.

1849 Anglo-Sikh wars rage in the Punjab, which becomes the final region of India to be annexed under a system of British rule that will persist for nearly a century.

1914– The Sikhs fight bravely and with great distinction alongside the
1945   British in both World Wars.

1947 Following the partition of this year, (Hindu) India and (predominantly Muslim) Pakistan emerge as separate nations—but dreams of an independent Punjabi-speaking Sikh nation are set aside. The period leading up to the partition was marked by great violence in the Punjab between Sikhs and Muslims. A grim migration of Punjabi Sikhs into present-day India followed; tensions between Sikhs and Hindus have been a persistent feature of modern life in the region.

Summary

- Sikhism's founding figure, Guru Nanak, both borrowed from and set his religious practice apart from Hinduism and Islam.

- Guru Nanak preached a distinctive monotheistic faith that was very closely tied to the peoples and culture of the Punjab.

- For a time, Sikhism was tolerated under the Mughal Empire of the Muslims; that ended when Guru Arjan, the sixth Guru, became the first Sikh martyr.

- Guru Gobind Singh became the tenth and final human Guru of Sikhism. He established the powerful military/religious institution known as the Khalsa and identified Sikhism's scripture as its perpetual eleventh Guru.

- The precepts, teachings, and principles of Sikhism are deeply interwoven with the history of the Punjab region.

QUIZ

1. **The founder of Sikhism was**
   A. Guru Angad.
   B. Guru Arjan.
   C. Guru Nanak.
   D. None of the above.

2. **Sikhism is most closely tied to the history and culture of the**
   A. Levant.
   B. Punjab.
   C. Arabian Peninsula.
   D. None of the above.

3. *Sikh* **means**
   A. "warrior."
   B. "Muslim."
   C. "student, disciple."
   D. None of the above.

4. *Guru* **means**
   A. "enlightened teacher."
   B. "Muslim sage."
   C. "Christian mystic."
   D. None of the above.

5. **The first Sikh martyr was killed by the**
   A. Mughals.
   B. Berbers.
   C. Ottomans.
   D. None of the above.

6. **The tenth Guru decreed that**
   A. his son would be the eleventh Guru.
   B. there would be no eleventh Guru.
   C. the Sikh holy scriptures would be the eleventh Guru.
   D. None of the above.

7. **In the years after the death of the tenth Guru, the Punjab**
    A. became entirely Muslim.
    B. became entirely Hindu.
    C. became entirely Christian.
    D. None of the above.

8. **Today, there are approximately**
    A. 1 million Sikhs.
    B. 5 million Sikhs.
    C. 30 million Sikhs.
    D. None of the above.

9. **True or false: All Muslim leaders persecuted the Sikhs.**

10. **True or false: The Sikhs fought alongside the British during the twentieth century.**

chapter **16**

Sikhism: Core Beliefs and Practices

Sikhism, a global faith, is closely tied to the culture and history of a single region, the Punjab. The belief system and ritual practices of this faith are best understood in the context of the adversities its adherents encountered as the faith developed in opposition to the Mughal Empire.

CHAPTER OBJECTIVES

In this chapter, you will learn about:

- What Sikhs believe
- The most important rituals and practices of Sikhism

Sikhism's belief system is remarkably free of both ambiguity and rancorous internal debate, at least in comparison with faiths such as Hinduism and Christianity. Let's take a close look at the essentials of this faith.

What Do Sikhs Believe?

One often runs the risk of oversimplifying matters by comparing one religion to another, but in the case of Sikhism, the comparisons are both unavoidable and unusually clear-cut. Hinduism, the name we use to describe the ancient and intricate pluralistic tradition of the Indian subcontinent, and Islam, the religion of the Mughal Empire, are competing traditions and inescapable contributors to the story of Sikh belief and practice. Sikhism arose in direct response to these two faiths, which predominated during the time of its founder, Guru Nanak. Sikhism borrowed from each and rejected aspects of each.

Sikhs believe in one eternal God. They dismiss the entire Hindu pantheon. They part company with Muslims in their insistence on the principle of reincarnation, which is central to Hinduism but which Islam rejects as heretical. Let's look more closely at the overlaps and the points of departure.

At its core, Sikhism is a rigorously monotheistic religion, believing in a single all-powerful God who created the universe and is formless and present in all things. This God, in the view of Sikhs, has never taken an express physical or human form, and human beings are fundamentally incapable of understanding God completely. In that respect, Sikh orthodoxy aligns closely with Islamic orthodoxy.

At the same time, however, Sikhs believe in a form of reincarnation that focuses on gathering truth over lifetimes. Such a principle is anathema to Muslims. What's more, Sikhs hold that the eventual goal of human beings is reaching complete understanding and truth, and thereby joining with God and ending the cycle of reincarnation. This fusing of the Creator with the Creation runs well afoul of mainstream Islamic practice and doctrine (although it has been the province of mystics in all faith systems).

The word *guru*, so important to Sikhism, is imported from Hinduism. The ten Gurus of Sikhism are revered as the guides on this journey toward knowing God, as is the *Guru Granth Sahib*, the Sikh holy scripture, which is, as we have seen, afforded the respect and obedience due to a living, human guru.

KEY TERMS DEMYSTIFIED: *Guru Granth Sahib*

The followers of Sikhism have a religious obligation to follow the teachings of the ten Sikh Gurus, or enlightened leaders. The tenth of this line, Guru Gobind Singh Ji, identified the Sikh scripture itself as the eleventh and perpetual Guru, the last Guru in the sequence. This is why the scripture bears the name *Guru Granth Sahib.*

The two core tenets of Sikhism are the ideas of Simran and Sewa. Simran is individual contemplation and meditation on God and yourself, in the hopes of understanding the Truth of God more completely. Sewa is similar to charity and requires service to others without consideration for oneself. In Sewa, the services are supposed to be rendered to God through connection to all people. This can take many forms, from formalized practices to individual moments of giving, and may be undertaken on any scale. These two ideas are the goals of all Sikh religious behavior, through which salvation is achieved.

The Sikh Gurus also detailed five evils or vices that lead humans farther from God or distract from the path to truth. These evils are lust (Kam), rage (Krodh), greed (Lobh), attachment (Moh), and ego (Ahankar). Sikhs are taught to be on guard against these at all times and refuse their influence.

SPIRITUALLY SPEAKING

"Like the mad dog running around in all directions, the greedy person, unaware, consumes everything, edible and non-edible alike. Engrossed in the intoxication of sexual desire and anger, people wander through reincarnation over and over again."

—*Guru Granth Sahib*

Standing contrast to the five evils are the five virtues, which bring humans closer to God. These are truth (Sat), compassion (Daya), contentment (Santokh), humility (Nimrata), and love (Pyare). By cultivating these virtues, Sikhs hold that they are bringing themselves closer to a full realization of God.

Sikhism is a deeply egalitarian religion and places a strong emphasis on equality. All human beings, regardless of their ethnic or religious identity, are regarded as equal to Sikhs, and, for instance, can make use of Sikh community services, such as community kitchens or other facilities. Within the Sikh faith, women are considered equals of men in all respects and are allowed to lead in worship. The Gurus preached against social practices like the mandatory wearing of veils, female infanticide, and pressuring widows to throw themselves onto the pyres of their dead husbands, all of which were common in India at the time.

Sikhs are taught to embody the virtues of the *Sant-Sipahi*, or "saint-soldier," by cultivating a love for and awareness of God, and by showing personal courage in the face of injustice. At the same time, it is important to note that Sikhism views human life as sacred, because it is the avenue through which oneness with God is achieved. Sikhs are expected to stand up to injustice and defend religious truth, but this defense is not necessarily undertaken through force. The tenth Sikh Guru, Guru Gobind Singh Ji, taught, "There is a right to use force as a last resort when all other peaceful means have failed."

Important Sikh Practices and Rituals

Guru Nanak established three core practices of Sikhism that serve as the foundation for the religion. First is Naam Japna, a kind of daily meditation and chanting of holy words, specifically the Name of God. Next is Kirat Karni, the practice of earnest living and application of your God-given abilities honestly and productively. Included in this is the fulfillment of family and social responsibilities to the fullest. Additionally, there is Vand Chakna, a type of community giving that entails sharing food, wealth, and other commodities within a community, often through a type of tithing, and charity outside a community to those in need.

Other widely observed practices within the faith include the following.

- **Baptism.** To enter into the congregation of the Sikh religion, the Khalsa, a person (male or female) has to undergo a ritual baptism. There is no specific age requirement, but one must be old enough to understand the commitment being made. After having gone through this ceremony, adherents of both genders are expected to wear the five articles of faith, often called the five Ks: uncut hair (kes), a knife or sword (kirpan), a circular piece of steel or a steel bracelet (kara), a special type of cotton undergarment (kacchera), and a wooden comb (kangha). These items each have an individual religious significance, and taken together mark the wearer as a Sikh.

- **Males wearing the Dastar (turban).** The distinctive turban, which covers uncut hair, is a mandatory article of apparel among baptized Sikh males. The headgear represents piety and courage, and is considered a central element of the distinctive Sikh identity. A tiny minority of Sikh women opt to wear it, as well. (It is worth noting here in passing that the Sikh turban has often been mistaken by outsiders for Muslim apparel—despite the fact that Muslim men are under no religious obligation to sport headgear of any kind.)

- **Observance of Sikh holidays.** The faith generally de-emphasizes festivals and other rites, yet a few important communal holidays have emerged and are widely observed. These include Bandi Chhor Divas, which celebrates the release of the sixth Guru from a Mughal prison, and Visakhi, which commemorates the inauguration of the Khalsa.

Sikh wearing the Dastar (turban).

Credit: Lissa Harrison

CAREFUL! *Although there is a proud military history among Sikhs, there was (and is) far more than a warrior code to explain the enduring faith of Sikhism. Its focus has always been on the cultivation of personal virtue in the context of supporting the larger community. Sikhs are obliged to seek justice in all matters, and are committed to the continuous reform of human society. They must control personal desires and make a clear commitment to a course of constant self-improvement, the kind of ongoing personal growth that brings into being the positive qualities outlined in the faith's holy text, the* **Guru Granth Sahib.**

Sikhism in a Box	
Divinity	Monotheistic.
Afterlife	Reincarnation until one's personal karma is resolved, at which point one attains unity with God.
Purpose of Human Life	Transcend selfish impulses, align with the will of God, and attain/ practice the virtues of the "saint-soldier." Defend the weak and oppressed, by force if necessary.
Distinctive Practices and Beliefs	Prayer and worship via meditation on the name of God; services held in gurdwara; the "five Ks"; males wear a turban. Charity and community work are strongly emphasized. Asceticism and monasticism are not endorsed.
Outsiders Often Distracted by	Supposed glorification of war and warriors. (In fact, the faith permits the use of military force only as a last resort.) Significance of the Dastar (turban), which has often led outsiders to confuse Sikhs with Muslims.

Summary

- Sikhism embraces the principles of monotheism and reincarnation. Sikhs are taught to embody the virtues of the Sant-Sipahi—"saint-soldier." Human life is sacred in Sikhism.

- Sikhs follow the teachings of the ten Sikh Gurus, or enlightened leaders. The tenth of this line, Guru Gobind Singh Ji, identified the Sikh scripture, the *Guru Granth Sahib*, itself as the eleventh and perpetual Guru.

- Important Sikh rituals and practices include baptism, the wearing of the "five Ks" (articles of religious devotion), and, for men, the mandatory wearing of the turban (Dastar).

- Sikhism is a deeply egalitarian religion and places a strong emphasis on gender equality.

QUIZ

1. **Sikhism arose in response to**

    A. Hinduism and Islam.

    B. Christianity and Judaism.

    C. Taoism and Shinto.

    D. All of the above.

2. **Sikhism differs from Hinduism in that it**

    A. rejects the Hindu pantheon.

    B. is not historically connected to the Indian subcontinent.

    C. embraces the sacrificial role of Jesus Christ.

    D. None of the above.

3. **Sikhism differs from Islam in that it**

    A. rejects monotheism.

    B. accepts the doctrine of reincarnation.

    C. prohibits its followers from engaging in battle.

    D. None of the above.

4. **The Sikh religious scripture is known as the**

    A. *Guru Nanak*.

    B. *Guru Granth Sahib*.

    C. *Guru Arjan*.

    D. None of the above.

5. **The two core tenets of Sikhism are**

    A. Simran and Sewa.

    B. Khalsa and Kirpan.

    C. Dastar and Bandi Chhor.

    D. None of the above.

6. **Sikhs are taught to embody the virtues of the *Sant-Sipahi*, which means**

    A. "statesman-citizen."

    B. "saint-soldier."

    C. "angel-God."

    D. None of the above.

7. **To enter into the congregation of the Sikh religion, one must be**
   A. old enough to understand the commitment being made in ritual baptism.
   B. twenty-one years old.
   C. thirty years old.
   D. None of the above.

8. **Sikhs wear articles of faith known as**
   A. the "five Ks."
   B. the "five Ss."
   C. the "five Bs."
   D. None of the above.

9. **A Sikh house of worship is known as a**
   A. mosque.
   B. synagogue.
   C. gurdwara.
   D. None of the above.

10. **True or false: Male Sikhs are required to wear a turban.**

Independent Belief Systems

In this chapter, we look at a representative sampling of influential belief movements, old and new, that are smaller and that operate independently of the larger traditions.

CHAPTER OBJECTIVES

In this chapter you will learn about:

- Atheism
- Agnosticism
- Nature-focused faith systems
- Jainism
- The Baha'i faith
- The Rastafari movement
- Santeria
- Candomblé

Each of the faith systems we have focused on in the previous chapters of this book established itself as the "majority" faith in at least one geographically or politically dominant human culture. It is natural enough that these "majority" faiths should attract interest from readers—and the most essay assignments from instructors. Yet these larger "majority" systems of belief are not the only important religious movements in human history. Let's look now at some of the influential "minority" belief systems.

Atheism

Atheism is a generalized term for disbelief in the existence of gods, deities, or other divine forces within the universe.

The term *atheism* comes from a Greek phrase meaning "without gods." This school of thought is usually contrasted with theism, the belief in one or more deities. As atheism is dependent on a rejection of religion, including centralized or organized religion, there are no core or common tenets. In recent years, however, atheists have become more open in expressing their views, particularly in pluralistic countries such as the United States and the United Kingdom. Prominent atheists such as the philosopher Peter Singer and the entertainer Penn Jillette have made a point of comparing and contrasting their perspective with those of the representatives of established religious movements.

Atheism argues that there is no need for a divine explanation for human existence, or existence in general. Individual atheists often differ on their precise arguments against the concept of divinity and their outlook on the world; by its very nature, atheism has no central teachings or dogma. Nevertheless there are several common strains of atheist argument related to this rejection of theistic belief, including the idea that rational human beings are fully capable of creating their own codes of proper conduct without divine guidance; the contention that modern science either disproves or makes obsolete the idea of a divine creator or divine beings; the inconsistency of a benevolent creator and a created world that includes evil; the fact that there are many religions claiming to be uniquely true; and the argument that if everything is created by means of a divine power, then that divine power itself must have been created, a pattern that falls into an infinite (and presumably illogical) loop.

Atheists are antireligious, but many follow humanist philosophies that emphasize the worth and capability of human beings. The lack of an organized dogma does not mean that atheists do not or cannot follow strict ethical codes. Instead, atheists argue, the lack of dogma means merely that they claim individual agency over those codes.

> ## KEY TERMS DEMYSTIFIED: **Humanism**
>
> A philosophical movement emphasizing the role and worth of human beings, both individually and collectively. Humanism tends to prefer individual thought and inquiry over organizational dogma or ritualized belief systems.

Agnosticism

Often connected with atheism is the (very different) theory of agnosticism, which is the belief that there is no way to actually prove or disprove the existence of divine forces.

While atheism actively asserts that there is no divine presence in the universe, agnosticism takes the view that it would be impossible to accurately conclude for or against the existence of such a presence. Agnostics are often described as those who "neither believe nor disbelieve" in God, though this view is somewhat limiting. It's probably more accurate to state that agnosticism is the contention that the human mind is not sufficiently capable of understanding or confirming divinity. Agnosticism actively acknowledges the unknowability of divine presence and places an emphasis instead on the concrete facts of the physical world.

Agnosticism is not an exclusive philosophy, and it is possible for an agnostic to also be a theist or an atheist. This is possible because agnosticism is more of a worldview than an individual philosophy, so an individual can choose to believe (or disbelieve) personally in a certain religion while acknowledging the agnostic principle that his or her faith (or lack of faith) can never be empirically justified.

Agnosticism is concerned, fundamentally, with emphasizing the difference between belief and truth. Like atheism, it has no central, organized doctrine or tenets, instead relying on other sources for codes of conduct.

Nature-Focused Faith Systems

There are many communities of nature-focused faith systems scattered across the world, often based on local traditional beliefs. These faiths are often grouped together using variations on the label *pagan*, though how that term is viewed is a complex topic that varies greatly from community to community and individual to individual. Some embrace the *pagan* or *neopagan* label, while others seek to avoid it and the religious and social baggage it carries.

Many of the faiths under the umbrella are based on, or claim to be based on, the practices of pre-Christian Europe, though the extent to which they admit or incorporate more modern influence also varies. Included in this grouping are faiths such as Wicca, which was developed in the twentieth century in Britain and is popularly associated with witchcraft and ritualistic magic, as well as various strains of Druidism, Shamanism, and other systems.

A common thread among these faiths is reverence for nature and the natural world; many of these faiths are poly- or pantheistic as well as animist. Additionally, these faiths often incorporate a revival of traditional folk culture and can be heavily influenced by the folklore and traditions of the area they are found in (not unlike Shinto).

Often the festivals, ceremonies, and holidays of these religions are based on the passage of agricultural seasons. While many individual faiths have their own scriptures and religious texts, there is no overarching book or teaching among them. There is often an emphasis on individualism and self-actualization. One of the most prominent and widespread ethical codes among the Pagan umbrella is the Wiccan Rede, which is commonly interpreted as "Do what you will, so long as it harms none."

A common thread within this group of beliefs is an implied or openly stated rejection of the perceived conformity required by Abrahamic faiths.

Jainism

Among the most ancient active religions in the world is Jainism, an Indian religion distinct from the Vedic tradition that spawned Hinduism. The religion claims something like four million followers worldwide, with the vast majority located in India.

Jains follow the teachings of the Tirthankara, the leaders of their faith. Parsva, the earliest Tirthankara who is accepted as a historical figure, dates from the ninth century BCE. However, it is widely accepted that Parsva is not the founder of Jainism, or even the first Tirthankara, and speculation links Jain tradition to some of the earliest archaeological sites in India.

Jainism follows a theology of pacifism and nonviolence, and espouses a supreme respect for all living things. Living a harmless life is among the strongest teachings of Jainism. Valuing the souls of all living things equally, Jainism places a strict prohibition on eating meat and emphasizes the efficient and ethical use of natural resources.

Like other Indian religions, Jainism teaches a cycle reincarnation that can be broken by cleansing the soul of karma. By breaking out of the cycle of reincarnation, Jains seek liberation and aim for their freed souls to live forever.

Jainism does not advocate the worship of any gods; the onus of salvation is placed on individual humans. The holy text of Jainism is the Agamas, which are the collected teachings of the last Tirthankara.

The Baha'i Faith

One of the youngest and fastest-growing world religions is the Baha'i faith, which can be traced to the mid-nineteenth century, and a man known as Bahá'u'lláh, who lived in what is now Iran.

Bahá'u'lláh proclaimed publicly that he was God's most recent Manifestation, and that his coming had been foretold by a previous Manifestation who had been known as the Bab. This announcement conflicted with the Shia Muslim religious authorities. To escape persecution for their beliefs, he and his son led a growing number of followers across the Middle East. After the death of Bahá'u'lláh's son in 1908, the leadership of the Baha'i faith passed to an elected representative government called the Universal House of Justice, located in what is now Israel. While this faith's governing body insists that it is not the head of a religious hierarchy, it does handle the religion's affairs and monitor its expansion.

Baha'i is an inclusive Universalist faith, proclaiming that all religions and all prophets are different manifestations of the same singular God. According to the Baha'i faith, each different religious revelation contains inspiration from the same God, made accessible to the unique situations and experiences of different peoples in different places and times according to God's benevolent and omniscient plan.

> ## KEY TERMS DEMYSTIFIED: **Universalism**
>
> The belief that there are religious, philosophical, and theological principles that have universal applicability, regardless of social or sectarian differences.

This faith is perhaps the most inclusive now in practice, explicitly claiming both Abrahamic and dharmic figures as true manifestations of God with valuable revelations. Followers of Baha'i are tasked with learning to love God, primarily through loving humankind. They incorporate aspects of prayer and rituals from many different faiths into their worship.

Baha'i theology places a strong emphasis on three unities: the unity of God, the unity of the believers, and the unity of humankind. Much of the faith's religious text takes the form of letters between individuals and communities, translated into many languages to better facilitate the faith's spread. There are about seven million followers of the Baha'i faith around the world. The faith is remarkably widespread and is growing rapidly.

The Rastafari Movement

Another comparatively young religious tradition is the Rastafari movement, which was founded in the 1930s in Jamaica.

Members of this movement, called Rastas, avoid the term *Rastafarianism*, as the concept of "-isms" in general is frowned on in Rasta theology. Rastas worship the late Haile Selassie I (1892–1974), the emperor of Ethiopia, either as the second coming of Jesus or as God the Father himself, depending on the denomination. Selassie himself was not a part of the Rasta movement and distanced himself from it.

The Rastafari movement is based loosely on Judeo-Christian traditions; they call God by the name Jah, a contraction of Jehovah. Its theology focuses on African culture, and preaches that Africans are God's chosen people, that their rightful place in society has been repressed by European intervention and suppression, and that one day they will be reinstated by Jah.

The Rastafari movement was spread worldwide by reggae music in the 1970s, and music has an extremely important place within Rasta culture and rituals. Rastas seek to reach high spiritual consciousness through forswearing material things, by following strict codes of behavior (including a prohibition on cutting hair), and through the sacramental use of marijuana. The material culture that the movement condemns, including the consumption of meat and alcohol, is often referred to as Babylon culture, and it is contrasted with the culture of Zion, which signifies Ethiopia. The movement calls for repatriation to Zion.

The Rastafari movement is not centralized or highly organized; there are several different sects, called Mansions, but many Rastas do not identify with these. There are about one million Rastas worldwide, and Rastas form a religious minority in Jamaica itself.

Santeria

Santeria is a Caribbean religion that mixes the beliefs of the Yoruba people from parts of Nigeria, Benin, and Togo in Africa with aspects of Roman Catholicism.

Santeria grew in Cuba and was spread elsewhere in the Caribbean region following the Cuban Revolution. Santeria teaches that there is a single god named Olodumare, but that there are other entities, analogous to Catholic Saints, called Orisha, who are powerful spirits. There are three central Orisha, each of which has its own unique characteristics, and many other minor ones. These Orisha require human worship and sacrifice. They are not immortal but wield great powers over the physical world.

There is no central organization or regimented theology to Santeria. It is defined by the rituals its followers practice. There is no written tradition for the faith; instead, it relies on an exacting and careful initiation process to pass along the rituals and beliefs from one practitioner to another. Santeria priests are called Santeros and Santeras, depending on their gender, and are considered to have control over Orisha.

There is a complex hierarchy of priests within the faith. The house, and the attendant shrine each priest builds within it, is central to the religion as a locus for rituals and spirituality.

Many Santeria rituals are focused on healing and cleansing, or other personal and practical effects. Due to the decentralized, home-based, and word-of-mouth nature of Santeria, it is difficult to estimate the faith's size. It has a significant folk following throughout the Caribbean region across many ethnic groups.

Candomblé

Candomblé is the best known of a group of Afro-Brazilian religions practiced in various regions of Brazil. Most of these religions have their roots in nineteenth-century slave societies whose members tried to make sense of their experiences of bondage and suffering. Candomblé is estimated to have roughly two million followers.

Candomblé insists on a hierarchy and initiation rituals that incorporate a strong ethical sense of the values of reciprocity and ancestral obligation. First initiations are followed up by more initiations to reinforce spiritual energies of both devotees and orixas (deities), which is also done through annual ceremonies honoring the various orixas.

Orixa(s) is the term for the deity(ies) of several Afro-Brazilian religions with distinct Yoruban roots in what is today the Yoruba ethnicity of Nigeria. Orixas act as intermediaries for the supreme being, Olodumare (Olorun), whose rule is over every living thing. Wielding immense power, Olodumare created orixas as carriers of an aspect of his sacred energy, which becomes personalized to devotees.

The key features of Afro-Brazilian religions are their emphasis on ritual and medicinal healing, mutual aid, and intense relationships to spiritual entities. Music and dance are crucial to all rituals in order to move the worshipper into different levels of consciousness. Possession and trance enable devotees to feel close to their orixas, with whom they establish a lifelong relationship. Orixas are consulted by way of an ancient form of divination called Ifa, where the answers to a petitioner's questions are contained in verses and parables. Orixas are also consulted through a possession ritual.

Summary

- *Atheism* is a generalized term for disbelief in the existence of gods, deities, or other divine forces within the universe.

- Agnosticism is the belief that there is no way to prove or disprove the existence of divine forces.

- There are many communities of nature-focused faith systems scattered across the world, often based on local traditional beliefs.

- Among the most ancient active religions in the world is Jainism, an Indian religion distinct from the Vedic tradition that spawned Hinduism.

- One of the youngest and fastest-growing world religions is the inclusive, monotheistic Baha'i faith.

- Another comparatively young religious tradition is the Rastafari movement, which was founded in the 1930s in Jamaica.

- Santeria is a Caribbean religion that mixes the beliefs of the Yoruba people from parts of Nigeria, Benin, and Togo in Africa with aspects of Roman Catholicism.

- Candomblé is the best known of a group of Afro-Brazilian religions practiced in various regions of Brazil that have their roots in nineteenth-century slave societies.

QUIZ

1. **A contemporary proponent of atheism is**
   A. Haile Salassie I.
   B. Bahá'u'lláh.
   C. Peter Singer.
   D. None of the above.

2. **Atheism and agnosticism are**
   A. identical.
   B. systems of monotheism.
   C. distinct belief systems.
   D. None of the above.

3. **Agnostics maintain that**
   A. God is manifest in all human existence.
   B. it is not possible to prove or disprove the existence of a divine force.
   C. God does not exist.
   D. None of the above.

4. **Nonscriptural nature-focused belief systems**
   A. practice a wide variety of rituals and hold varying beliefs.
   B. are governed by a single administrative council headquartered in Israel.
   C. accept Jesus Christ as the Lord and Savior of all practitioners.
   D. None of the above.

5. **Most practitioners of Jainism are located in**
   A. Iran.
   B. South America.
   C. India.
   D. None of the above.

6. **The first followers of the Baha'i faith were located in**
   A. Iran.
   B. South America.
   C. India.
   D. None of the above.

7. **Among the most inclusive of all contemporary religions is**

    A. Santeria.

    B. the Baha'i faith.

    C. the Rastafari movement.

    D. None of the above.

8. **The Rastafari movement originated in**

    A. Jamaica.

    B. Brazil.

    C. Iran.

    D. None of the above.

9. **Santeria mixes the beliefs of the African Yoruba with aspects of**

    A. Roman Catholicism.

    B. Judaism.

    C. Islam.

    D. None of the above.

10. **Candomblé is practiced in various regions of**

    A. Cuba.

    B. Brazil.

    C. Nigeria.

    D. All of the above.

PART THREE TEST

In this part of the book, you will test your mastery of dissenting voices as you prepare for the Final Exam. You will also identify which, if any, of the independent religious traditions you've just studied should be reviewed more closely before you tackle that test.

1. **The word *gurdwara* means**
   A. "gateway to the Guru."
   B. "gateway to Islam."
   C. "gateway to the fog."
   D. None of the above.

2. ***Guru Granth Sahib* is**
   A. Sikhism's holy scripture.
   B. Sikhism's eleventh Guru.
   C. a collection of teachings from various periods.
   D. All of the above.

3. **Udasis were**
   A. sentences of death passed against the rulers of the Mughal Empire.
   B. important missionary journeys undertaken by Guru Nanak in order to spread his spiritual message.
   C. restrictions on headwear during religious festivals.
   D. None of the above.

4. **Simram describes**
   A. the acquisition of personal wealth that need not be shared with the community.
   B. a commitment to individual contemplation and meditation on both God and yourself, in the hopes of understanding the Truth of God more completely.
   C. a strategy for urban battle during wartime.
   D. None of the above.

5. **Sewa requires**
   A. service to others without consideration for oneself.
   B. solitary meditation.
   C. accreditation as a religious scholar.
   D. None of the above.

6. *Kam* means

    A. "truth."

    B. "lust."

    C. "balance."

    D. None of the above.

7. *Krodh* means

    A. "rage."

    B. "forgetfulness."

    C. "fortitude."

    D. None of the above.

8. *Lobh* means

    A. "music."

    B. "contemplation."

    C. "greed."

    D. None of the above.

9. *Moh* means

    A. "attachment."

    B. "resistance."

    C. "prayer."

    D. None of the above.

10. *Ahankar* means

    A. "selflessness."

    B. "ego."

    C. "community."

    D. None of the above.

11. *Sat* means

    A. "truth."

    B. "falsehood."

    C. "immobility."

    D. None of the above.

12. *Daya* means
    A. "harshness."
    B. "compassion."
    C. "poetic skill."
    D. None of the above.

13. *Santokh* means
    A. "restlessness."
    B. "pacifism."
    C. "contentment."
    D. None of the above.

14. *Nimrata* means
    A. "humility."
    B. "cleanliness."
    C. "meditation."
    D. None of the above.

15. *Pyare* means
    A. "hatred."
    B. "certainty."
    C. "love."
    D. None of the above.

16. **Sikhs are taught to embody the virtues of the _____ by cultivating a love for and awareness of God, and by showing personal courage in the face of injustice.**
    A. Sant-Sipahi
    B. Kes
    C. Kirpan
    D. Kara

17. **A Dastar is a**
    A. knife.
    B. undergarment.
    C. turban.
    D. None of the above.

18. **Atheism differs from agnosticism because**
    A. agnostics reject belief in one or more deities, but atheists maintain that certainty on such issues is impossible.
    B. atheists reject belief in one or more deities, but agnostics maintain that certainty on such issues is impossible.
    C. agnostics only share their beliefs with those who already agree with them, but atheists promote their beliefs to people of all kinds.
    D. None of the above.

19. **Humanism is**
    A. a philosophical movement emphasizing the role and worth of human beings, both individually and collectively.
    B. a religion based on the worship of human beings chosen at random.
    C. a political party.
    D. None of the above.

20. **Nature-focused faith systems are sometimes described as**
    A. Judeo-Christian.
    B. atheistic.
    C. pagan or neopagan.
    D. All of the above.

21. **Jainism is**
    A. among the most ancient active religions in the world.
    B. an Indian religion distinct from the Vedic tradition that spawned Hinduism.
    C. based on a theology of pacifism and nonviolence, with a supreme respect for all living things.
    D. All of the above.

22. **The Baha'i faith is**
    A. a denomination of Islam recognized by a majority of both Sunni and Shia scholars.
    B. an inclusive universalist faith, proclaiming that all religions and all prophets are different manifestations of the same singular God.
    C. a fifteenth-century response to Hinduism.
    D. None of the above.

23. **The Rastafari movement**
    A. is based loosely on Judeo-Christian traditions.
    B. refers to God by the name Jah.
    C. preaches a theology based on African culture.
    D. All of the above.

24. **Santeria is**
    A. a Brazilian religion that emphasizes the values of reciprocity and ancestral obligation.
    B. a Caribbean religion that mixes the beliefs of the African Yoruba people with aspects of Roman Catholicism.
    C. an Asian religion emphasizing solitary meditation and seclusion.
    D. None of the above.

25. **Candomblé is**
    A. a Brazilian religion that emphasizes the values of reciprocity and ancestral obligation.
    B. a Caribbean religion that mixes the beliefs of the African Yoruba people with aspects of Roman Catholicism.
    C. an Asian religion emphasizing solitary meditation and seclusion.
    D. None of the above.

Final Exam

1. **The word** *Hindu* **derives from**

   A. the Indus River.

   B. Indiana.

   C. Indigo.

   D. None of the above.

2. **The label** *Hinduism* **was coined by**

   A. Indian nationalists of the twentieth century.

   B. Pakistani nationalists of the twentieth century.

   C. outsiders who did not live on the Indian subcontinent.

   D. None of the above.

3. **Reincarnation refers to**

   A. the belief that you only go around once in life.

   B. the belief in the rebirth of the soul in a new body after death.

   C. the belief that life is meaningless.

   D. None of the above.

4. **True or false: Hinduism has a single recognized founding figure.**

5. **Hinduism's interactions with various cultures**

   A. did not take place.

   B. are uncertain.

   C. played a major role in the formation of the religion.

   D. None of the above.

6. **Within Hindu belief, karma is seen as**

   A. action that triggers inevitable good or bad results for the person who performs the action, either in this life or in a later incarnation.

   B. a kind of narcotic.

   C. a Christian doctrine.

   D. None of the above.

7. **Dharma refers to**

   A. a Mexican poetry movement.

   B. a kind of nomadic trance.

   C. one's personal spiritual obligations; it is seen as having no beginning and no end.

   D. None of the above.

8. **Shaivism, also known as Saivism,**

   A. is not technically part of Hinduism.

   B. is an English innovation.

   C. reveres the god Shiva as "creator, preserver, destroyer, revealer, and concealer of all that is."

   D. None of the above.

9. **The Vedas are**

   A. the oldest surviving examples of Indian literature and the oldest scriptures of Hinduism.

   B. written in Latin.

   C. a nineteenth-century response to British rule.

   D. None of the above.

10. **Brahma is**

    A. a Hindu god.

    B. a Hindu caste.

    C. a Massachusetts social class.

    D. None of the above.

11. **Vaishnavism, also known as Vaisnavism,**

    A. was developed in the 1920s.

    B. reveres the god Vishnu and his many manifestations as the original and all-powerful God.

    C. has never been practiced outside of India.

    D. None of the above.

12. **Shaktism holds as its object of veneration**

    A. a Catholic missionary.

    B. a certain literary technique from the Indian Golden Age.

    C. the ancient goddess figure Shakti, also known as Devi or Parvati, the Divine Mother.

    D. None of the above.

13. **The word *Buddha* means**

    A. "awakened one" or "enlightened one."

    B. "forgotten one."

    C. "hungry one."

    D. None of the above.

14. **An ethical religion is one that**

    A. only produces ethical followers.

    B. deemphasizes belief in a deity and instead promotes ethical and moral principles.

    C. creates missionary settlements.

    D. None of the above.

15. **Tradition tells us the Buddha was**

   A. a prince born in an area we would today call Nepal, near the northern Indian border.

   B. a military hero.

   C. a third-generation Zen master.

   D. None of the above.

16. **Before he was known as the Buddha, the central figure of Buddhism was known as**

   A. Vishnu.

   B. Shiva.

   C. Siddhartha Gautama.

   D. None of the above.

17. **An ascetic is someone who**

   A. abstains from all indulgence.

   B. eats as much as possible.

   C. creates chaos wherever he goes.

   D. None of the above.

18. **Buddhist tradition tells us that the Buddha's mind calmed and all became clear as he**

   A. hummed a simple tune.

   B. recited the works of a gifted poet.

   C. meditated beneath the bodhi tree.

   D. None of the above.

19. *Theravada* **means**

   A. "beyond knowledge."

   B. "evanescence."

   C. "doctrine of the elders."

   D. None of the above.

20. *Mahayana* means

    A. "great vehicle."

    B. "lesser vehicle."

    C. "diamond-studded vehicle."

    D. None of the above.

21. **Theravada Buddhists consider the Buddha a human being who, through human striving**

    A. died in atonement for inborn human sin.

    B. accumulated a great fortune.

    C. obtained Nirvana, a state beyond suffering.

    D. None of the above.

22. **Some Buddhists from the Mahayana school believe the Buddha**

    A. was born for the benefit of other beings.

    B. was not gifted with a physical form.

    C. was identical in appearance to the Jewish prophet David.

    D. None of the above.

23. **The Zen school of Buddhism emphasizes**

    A. commercialism and materialism.

    B. authenticity, self-control, and discipline.

    C. discovery of a new continent.

    D. None of the above.

24. **Vajrayana Buddhism is also known as**

    A. Japanese Buddhism.

    B. American Buddhism.

    C. Tibetan Buddhism.

    D. None of the above.

25. **Buddhists believe that the human perspective and personality, like every-thing else, is subject to being dissolved and even recombined with other elements during the process of**

   A. reincarnation.

   B. transsubstantiation.

   C. resurrection on the Day of Judgment.

   D. None of the above.

26. **True or False: One Buddhist conception of the law of karma holds that the potential energy of reproductive karma can be reversed by the more dominant opposing karma of the past.**

27. **A bodhisattva, in Buddhism, is generally understood to be an enlightened being who is able to reach Nirvana, but who foregoes Nirvana in order to**

   A. save suffering beings.

   B. save food.

   C. avoid delay in the fulfillment of monastic chores.

   D. None of the above.

28. **The Four Noble Truths hold that suffering exists, that it has causes, that it ends when one is freed from attachment and delusion, and that to end suffering one may**

   A. follow the Fourfold Path.

   B. follow the Sixfold Path.

   C. follow the Eightfold Path.

   D. None of the above.

29. **The *Tao* can be defined as**

   A. "deep attachment."

   B. "unsound personal financial planning."

   C. "the fundamental principle underlying the universe, 'the way things are.'"

   D. None of the above.

30. *Wu-wei* is a central concept in Taoism that literally means
    A. "action" or "doing."
    B. "literary creativity."
    C. "nonaction" or "nondoing."
    D. None of the above.

31. **True or False: The *Tao Te Ching* is the world's shortest religious text.**

32. **The *Tao Te Ching* is traditionally attributed to a sage known as**
    A. Lao-tzu.
    B. Zhuangzi.
    C. Dogen.
    D. None of the above.

33. **The second great text of Taoism is known as**
    A. the Zone.
    B. the Bonsai.
    C. the *Zhuangzi*.
    D. None of the above.

34. **The second text of Taoism advocates**
    A. violence toward one's subordinates.
    B. escape from the pressures of society.
    C. the accumulation of political power and wealth.
    D. None of the above.

35. **Taoism is probably best understood as**
    A. an exclusively religious tradition.
    B. an exclusively philosophical tradition.
    C. a hybrid of religious and philosophical traditions.
    D. None of the above.

36. **Religious Taoism, unlike philosophical Taoism, integrates significant elements from**

    A. Japanese folk culture.

    B. Chinese folk culture.

    C. Korean folk culture.

    D. None of the above.

37. **For millennia, Chinese thought has emphasized the importance of humanity's intimate connection to**

    A. nature and the universe.

    B. artificial cooling systems.

    C. music.

    D. None of the above.

38. **Direct experience of the Tao is the objective of such religious practices as breathing exercises, massage, martial arts, and**

    A. underwater exploration of the Australian Barrier Reef.

    B. newspaper curation.

    C. meditation

    D. None of the above.

39. **In religious Taoism, there are two types of "alchemy," namely**

    A. upper and lower.

    B. external and internal.

    C. inner and outer.

    D. None of the above.

40. **In Chinese thought, chi is**

    A. a traditional variety of vinegar.

    B. a sacramental expression of the body of Christ.

    C. an angel.

    D. None of the above.

41. Chi is the

    A. foundation principle of all traditional Chinese medicine and martial arts.

    B. sauce most commonly served with poultry.

    C. dominant historical movement advocating the restoration of ancient Chinese musical instruments.

    D. None of the above.

42. Shinto is the

    A. indigenous spiritual practice of the people of Japan.

    B. indigenous spiritual practice of the people of Korea.

    C. indigenous spiritual practice of the people of China.

    D. None of the above.

43. There are at least three competing views of the

    A. historical development of Shinto.

    B. birth of the Buddha in Japan.

    C. origin of Christianity in Japan.

    D. None of the above.

44. Shinto incorporates significant elements from the

    A. Christian Bible.

    B. Japanese animist faith systems of prehistory.

    C. Indonesian dance tradition.

    D. None of the above.

45. From about the sixth century of the Common Era forward, traditional belief systems in Japan faced major competition from

    A. Mormonism.

    B. Islam.

    C. Buddhism.

    D. None of the above.

46. **The centralized Shintoism of the Meiji era, which emphasized the divinity of the emperor, was abandoned after**

    A. the establishment of commercial ties with Europe.

    B. the creation of the first assembly line.

    C. Japan's defeat in World War II.

    D. None of the above.

47. **Confucian and Buddhist philosophy and tradition**

    A. have been banned in contemporary Japan.

    B. have replaced Shinto in contemporary Japan.

    C. coexist with Shinto in contemporary Japan.

    D. None of the above.

48. **Kami are**

    A. an endangered animal species worshipped by some Japanese.

    B. phenomena or spirits regarded as objects of worship within the religion of Shinto.

    C. a kind of video representation of spiritual ideals.

    D. None of the above.

49. **One recognizable symbol of Shinto is the gatelike structure known as a**

    A. borii.

    B. morii.

    C. torii.

    D. None of the above.

50. **True or false: The Shinto priesthood is open to both men and women.**

51. **Monotheism is**

    A. the worship of all manifestations of nature.

    B. the worship of a single God.

    C. the worship of multiple gods.

    D. None of the above.

52. **True or false: Judaism is the first recorded monotheistic religion.**

53. **Major faith systems whose adherents describe themselves as monotheistic include**
    A. Shinto.
    B. Judaism, Christianity, and Islam.
    C. Agnosticism.
    D. None of the above.

54. **The great first patriarch of the monotheistic tradition was**
    A. Samuel.
    B. Abraham.
    C. Noah.
    D. None of the above.

55. **The Tanakh is the distinctive Hebrew term for Judaism's core religious scriptures, beginning with the book of Genesis and ending with the book of**
    A. Chronicles.
    B. Exodus.
    C. Numbers.
    D. None of the above.

56. **A covenant is a**
    A. binding agreement.
    B. divorce.
    C. forgotten principle of US constitutional law.
    D. None of the above.

57. **Narratives of the Hebrew prophet Moses associate him with**
    A. the Acts of the Apostles.
    B. the Great Flood.
    C. the Ten Commandments.
    D. None of the above.

58. **European Jews were frequently attacked by Christian armies who were on the way to Jerusalem during**

    A. the Crusades.

    B. the First World War.

    C. the Second World War.

    D. None of the above.

59. **Jews were expelled from Spain in**

    A. 1292.

    B. 1392.

    C. 1492.

    D. None of the above.

60. **Widespread persecution and violence against Jews took place in, among other places,**

    A. Asia.

    B. Central Europe and Russia.

    C. the Caribbean.

    D. None of the above.

61. *Orthopraxy* **means**

    A. "correctness in belief."

    B. "heresy."

    C. "correctness in action or practice."

    D. None of the above.

62. **True or False: The Golden Rule appears prominently in the Jewish religious tradition, as well as in that of Christianity, Islam, Buddhism, and Hinduism.**

63. **While Aramaic was the ancient spoken language used by Jews in Babylonia and Israel, Hebrew was the language used for**

    A. communication with Rome.

    B. travel beyond the Levant.

    C. liturgy.

    D. None of the above.

64. **Kabbalah derives from a set of secret oral traditions that was standardized and spread among**

  A. Jews during the Middle Ages in Europe.

  B. Jews during the American Civil War.

  C. Christians during the Middle Ages in Europe.

  D. None of the above.

65. **Of the major modern Jewish movements, Orthodox Judaism is**

  A. the least traditional in its practices.

  B. the most traditional in its practices.

  C. the most committed to gender equality during religious services.

  D. None of the above.

66. **The Reform movement of modern Judaism emerged from Germany in the early 1800s and was a response to**

  A. Zionism.

  B. the Protestant Reformation.

  C. the perceived legalism of mainstream Judaism of that time.

  D. None of the above.

67. **Conservative Judaism, also known as Masorti Judaism, is a moderate movement that tries to**

  A. attract converts from Christianity and Islam.

  B. celebrate the principle of political engagement.

  C. avoid the perceived extremes of Orthodox and Reform Judaism.

  D. None of the above.

68. **The historical existence of Jesus is**

  A. acknowledged by virtually all historians of antiquity.

  B. denied by virtually all historians of antiquity.

  C. a matter of dispute among contemporary Christians.

  D. None of the above.

69. *Apostle* is a Greek word meaning

   A. "anointed one."

   B. "emissary."

   C. "Divine One."

   D. None of the above.

70. In the earliest years of the Christian Church, believers often faced opposition from

   A. Muslim invaders.

   B. Hindu politicians.

   C. the Roman authorities, who blamed Christians for the Great Fire of Rome.

   D. None of the above.

71. After the turn of the first century of the Common Era, Christianity entered a phase that came to be known as the

   A. bi-Nicene period.

   B. post-Nicene period.

   C. duo-Nicene period.

   D. None of the above.

72. Emperor Constantine I personally embraced Christianity and issued the Edict of Milan in 313 CE that

   A. officially legalized Christianity within the Roman Empire.

   B. banned all faiths other than Christianity.

   C. formulated the doctrine of the Trinity.

   D. None of the above.

73. The Nicene Creed was originally formulated in 325 CE and was revised in 381 CE at

   A. the Council of Rome.

   B. the Council of Constantinople.

   C. the Council of Antioch.

   D. None of the above.

74. **After the fall of the Western Roman Empire, the Christian Church became a major center of culture and stability in the lives of**

   A. Western Europeans.

   B. Eastern Europeans.

   C. Asians.

   D. None of the above.

75. **The Great Schism of 1054 was the culmination of a complex series of disagreements that**

   A. sparked the Protestant Reformation.

   B. ended the Western Roman Empire.

   C. led the Roman Church to excommunicate the Eastern Patriarchy, and vice versa.

   D. None of the above.

76. **The Pope is the**

   A. Bishop of Rome and the global leader of the Catholic Church.

   B. lowest-ranking Cardinal.

   C. highest-ranking Protestant.

   D. None of the above.

77. **In 1517, a monk named Martin Luther issued 95 theses, or scholarly arguments, condemning various practices of the Roman Catholic Church, and in so doing**

   A. excommunicated the Eastern Patriarchy.

   B. sparked the Protestant Reformation.

   C. founded the Church of Jesus Christ of Latter-day Saints.

   D. None of the above.

78. **Major branches of Christianity after the Protestant Reformation include the Anglican Church, the Presbyterian Church, and the**

   A. Methodist Church.

   B. Eastern Orthodox Church.

   C. Ottoman Empire.

   D. None of the above.

79. **The Trinity is an important doctrine of mainstream Christianity identifying**

    A. "one God in three persons."

    B. Jesus, Mary, and Joseph.

    C. Abraham, Moses, and Aaron.

    D. None of the above.

80. **Reverence for and obedience to the teachings of Jesus Christ is**

    A. formally regarded as "optional" for most Catholics.

    B. a "nonnegotiable" of the Christian faith.

    C. a violation of the Lord's Prayer.

    D. None of the above.

81. **Among the most celebrated and powerful words attributed to Jesus are the Beatitudes, which**

    A. can be found in the book of Genesis.

    B. are not included in the New Testament.

    C. begin the account of the Sermon on the Mount found in the Gospel of Matthew.

    D. None of the above.

82. **The Christian Communion ritual mirrors Gospel accounts of**

    A. the parting of the Red Sea.

    B. the Great Flood.

    C. Jesus's Last Supper.

    D. None of the above.

83. **Communion is usually an essential element of**

    A. Hanukkah.

    B. Kwanzaa.

    C. weekly Christian communal worship services.

    D. None of the above.

84. **Important Christian holidays include Good Friday, Easter, and**

    A. Passover.

    B. Christmas.

    C. Eid.

    D. None of the above.

85. The word *Islam* originates from the Arabic root S-L-M, which means roughly

    A. "to be safe and free."

    B. "worship the moon."

    C. "migrate."

    D. None of the above.

86. The center of the new religion that arose in seventh-century Arabia was the city of

    A. Casablanca.

    B. Mecca.

    C. Yathrib.

    D. None of the above.

87. Muslims view Muhammad as the

    A. "seal of the prophets."

    B. first and only Prophet of God.

    C. Divine Creator.

    D. None of the above.

88. The Muslim holy scripture is known as the

    A. Qur'an.

    B. *Tae Te Ching*.

    C. New Testament.

    D. None of the above.

89. True or false: The Prophet Muhammad's central message stressed the triune nature of Allah, "one God in three persons."

90. After a plot to kill Muhammad failed, he led an exodus with his family and a few followers to

    A. Cairo.

    B. Jerusalem.

    C. Tripoli.

    D. None of the above.

91. **After several encounters between his forces and those of the Meccan army, the Prophet Muhammad took over the city of Mecca**

    A. by slaughtering half of the population of the city.

    B. after a prolonged siege.

    C. in a maneuver without bloodshed.

    D. None of the above.

92. **In 632, the last year of his life, the Prophet Muhammad led the first Islamic pilgrimage to Mecca and delivered**

    A. the authentic version of the Gospel.

    B. his historic Farewell Pilgrimage speech.

    C. a private address to the Meccan elite.

    D. None of the above.

93. **The six articles of Islamic faith do NOT include**

    A. worship of Jesus Christ as the Son of God.

    B. prayer.

    C. fasting during Ramadan.

    D. None of the above.

94. **The founder of Sikhism is known as**

    A. Guru Maharaj-Ji.

    B. Guru Nanak.

    C. Guru Dev.

    D. None of the above.

95. **A gurdwara is a**

    A. Muslim temple.

    B. Sikh house of worship.

    C. Taoist mosque.

    D. None of the above.

96. **Sikhism is intimately connected with the region known as the**

    A. Punjab.

    B. Gobi.

    C. Sahara.

    D. None of the above.

97. **Sikhism endorses the doctrine of**

    A. reincarnation.

    B. polytheism.

    C. Islam.

    D. None of the above.

98. **True or false: Female Sikhs are prohibited from leading religious service.**

99. **Atheism is**

    A. illegal in the United States.

    B. permitted in Orthodox Judaism.

    C. a generalized term for disbelief in the existence of gods, deities, or other divine forces within the universe.

    D. None of the above.

100. **Agnosticism is**

    A. the belief that there is no way to prove or disprove the existence of divine forces.

    B. a strain of the Rastafari movement.

    C. identical with Mormonism.

    D. None of the above.

Glossary

Advent The four Sundays before Christmas, devoted to preparation for that holiday and for the Second Coming of Christ. (Christianity)

Agnosticism The belief that there is no way to prove or disprove the existence of divine forces.

Ahankar Ego, one of the five evils or vices that lead humans further from God and distracts from the path to truth. (Sikhism)

Allah The Arabic word for "God." It appears in pre-Islamic texts (for instance, those of Arabian Christians) as the name of the God of Abraham. (Islam)

Animism The belief that naturally occurring entities—such as plants, animals, or other elements or phenomena—are worthy of worship and/or reverence, due to the spiritual essence they possess.

Apostle A Greek word meaning "emissary." The term may be taken to mean one of the original Jewish followers of Jesus commissioned to spread the good news of his ministry (among whom were Simon Peter, the "rock" on which Jesus proclaimed that the Church would be built, and John, the "disciple whom Jesus loved"). The word may also be used to include later converts such as Paul of Tarsus, the "apostle to the Gentiles" (Romans 11:13). (Christianity)

The Apostle Paul The most successful Christian missionary of the first-century world. He founded Christian churches in Asia Minor and Europe, and skillfully used his status as a Jew and a citizen of the Roman Empire to support his ministry. (Christianity)

Ascetic Someone who abstains from all indulgence.

Atheism Comes from a Greek phrase meaning "without gods." This school of thought rejects the belief in one or more deities. As atheism is dependent on a rejection of religion, including centralized or organized religion, there are no core or common tenets.

The Baha'i faith An inclusive Universalist faith proclaiming that all religions and all prophets are different manifestations of the same singular God. One of the fastest-growing new religious movements.

Bar mitzvah A coming-of-age ceremony for Jewish boys who reach their thirteenth birthday. The female equivalent is a **bat mitzvah**. (Judaism)

Bhagavad Gita An excerpt from the epic text known as the *Mahabharata*, regarded as one of the masterpieces of world literature. The text of the *Bhagavad Gita* presents the Lord Krishna as a divine teacher, in discussion with the prince Arjuna. (Hinduism)

Bhakti The active, loving devotional activity of a worshipper toward the divine. (Hinduism)

Bhakti Yoga A spiritual, mental, and physical discipline incorporating a personal attitude of love and devotion toward the Divine. (Hinduism)

Brahma The Hindu god of creation. Not to be confused with *Brahman, Brahmin*. (Hinduism)

Brahman The Hindu concept of the supreme spirit that transcends, is the origin of, and is the means of support for, the universe. Not to be confused with *Brahma, Brahmin*. (Hinduism)

Brahmin A member of the highest caste, or social class, within Indian society. Not to be confused with *Brahma, Brahman*. (Hinduism)

Buddha The word means "Awakened One" or "Enlightened One," and also describes the central figure of *Buddhism*.

Buddhism A religion encompassing beliefs and practices attributed to the *Buddha*.

Candomblé The best known of a group of Afro-Brazilian religions practiced in various regions of Brazil. Candomblé insists on a hierarchy and on initiation rituals that incorporate a strong ethical sense of the values of reciprocity and ancestral obligation.

Chi gung Also called qigong, this is the traditional Taoist practice of aligning breath, movement, and mindfulness for healing, exercise, and meditation. Qigong derives from ancient principles found in Chinese medicine, martial arts, and philosophy, and is understood by the practitioner as a means of cultivating and balancing chi (qi). (Taoism)

Christianity A monotheistic religion based on the New Testament's presentation of the life and teachings of Jesus Christ.

Christmas. Observed on December 25, this holiday celebrates the birth of Jesus. (Christianity)

Confucianism An important ethical and philosophical system based on the principles of the ancient Chinese philosopher Master Kong, known more commonly in the contemporary West as Confucius.

Conservative Judaism (also known as Masorti Judaism outside the United States) A moderate movement that tries to avoid the extremes of Orthodox and Reform Judaism. In keeping with the name, Conservative Jews want to conserve certain traditional elements of Judaism while also allowing for modernization. (Judaism)

Dastar This distinctive turban, which covers uncut hair, is a mandatory article of apparel among baptized Sikh males.

Daya Compassion, one of the five virtues that bring humans closer to God. (Sikhism)

Denominations in Islam Sunni Muslims, the majority group, make up between 75 and 90 percent of the global body of Muslim believers; Shia Muslims constitute between 10 and 20 percent of the total. (There are other denominations, as well, and subgroups within the Sunni and Shia groups.) Shia Muslims form majorities in countries such as Iran and Iraq. Both groups accept the Qur'an as the unerring, literal word of God, but there are important differences between the two. The differences—cultural, historical, and scholarly—are stark and significant, and extend deep into Islamic history. A core disagreement between the two denominations concerns the nephew of the Prophet, Ali, regarded by Shia Muslims as the divinely appointed successor of the Prophet Muhammad and the first rightful Imam (leader) of the faithful. Sunni Muslims accept Ali as an exemplary role model and a rightly guided Caliph (successor), but reject the notion that he was designated by Muhammad before his death as the rightful next leader of the Muslims. (Islam)

Dharma The word overs a wide range of meanings. In most modern contexts, it can refer either to one's personal spiritual obligations based on factors such as age, social class, or gender, to one's capacity for upright behavior, or simply to one's religion. The word also carries an ancient meaning of "that which upholds or supports." One translation of the critical phrase *Sanātana Dharma* might be "the eternal law that preserves." Dharma is seen as having no beginning and no end. (Buddhism, Hinduism)

Easter The most important Christian holiday, this holiday celebrates the resurrection of Jesus. (Christianity)

The Eightfold Path The subject of Buddhism's Fourth Noble Truth and the doctrinal heart of Buddhism. It is a process, not a set of rules. (Buddhism)

Ema Small wooden plaques Shinto believers use to record written supplications. They are then left at a shrine in the hope that kami will receive them. (Shinto)

Ethical religion One that emphasizes the pursuit of virtuous or exemplary behavior over a belief in a deity. Buddhism, Taoism, and Confucianism have been classified as ethical religions.

External alchemy The art of mastering special breathing techniques, sexual practices, physical exercises, and yoga, and even attempting to produce an elixir for longevity and/or immortality. (Taoism)

The Five Ks Uncut hair (kes), a knife or sword (kirpan), a circular piece of steel or a steel bracelet (kara), a special type of cotton undergarment (kacchera), and a wooden comb (kangha). These items each have an individual religious significance, and taken together mark the wearer as a Sikh. (Sikhism)

The Five Precepts Buddhism's five basic guidelines by which to live. The Five Precepts are recommendations, not inviolable rules. Individual Buddhists are meant to use their own discretion and experience in determining exactly how to implement these five guidelines.

The Four Noble Truths These four concepts examine the source and remedy for human suffering. (Buddhism)

The Golden Rule This principle appears prominently in the Jewish religious tradition, as well as in that of Christianity, Islam, Buddhism, Hinduism, and other influential faith systems. In its various expressions, the Golden Rule maintains that what one would wish to experience personally should guide the behavior one employs in interactions with others.

Good Friday This holiday observes the day when Jesus was crucified. (Christianity)

The Great Schism of 1054 In the history of Christianity, the culmination of a series of disagreements over authority on a number of complex religious and political issues. It led the Roman Church to excommunicate the Eastern Patriarchy, and vice versa. Prior to the schism, the Eastern and Western strands of the Christian faith had been different but had generally had cordial relations. After it, the two Churches formally accused each other of heresy. (Christianity)

Gurdwara A Sikh house of worship. The name means "gateway to the Guru." The structure is easily recognizable, thanks to tall flagpoles flying the Sikh flag. People from all faiths are welcome within a gurdwara. (Sikhism)

Guru A wise person with experience and authority in a certain area of human affairs. The word means "enlightened leader." (Hinduism, Sikhism)

Guru Granth Sahib Sikhism's holy scripture and its perpetual eleventh Guru. (Sikhism)

Hajj The mandatory pilgrimage to Mecca. It is to be undertaken at least once in a lifetime by each and every Muslim. Those who live far away from Mecca and cannot afford the journey are excused, but are encouraged to find the means and to make a prayerful commitment to complete the journey in the future. (Islam)

Hebrew While Aramaic was the ancient spoken language used by Jews in Babylonia and Israel, Hebrew was the language used for recording written language and remains the formal language of liturgy for many Jews. The *Torah* was originally written in Hebrew. (Judaism)

Hinduism The long legacy, and new expression, of religious tradition originating in and around India, from at least the Iron Age forward.

Humanism A philosophical movement emphasizing the role and worth of human beings, both individually and collectively. Humanism tends to prefer individual thought and inquiry over organizational dogma or ritualized belief systems.

Indus River Valley Civilization A civilization (3300 BCE to 1500 BCE) comprising some of the biggest human habitations of the ancient world. It was located in sections of present-day Pakistan and India. (Hinduism)

Internal alchemy Includes refined visualization, stringent dieting, precise sexual exercises, and sexual restraint. A strict diet is believed to kill demons within the body and stimulates and maintains energy. The many different types of meditation all revolve around breathing disciplines. (Taoism)

Islam The word originates from the Arabic root S-L-M, which means roughly "to be safe and free." The infinitive for Islam means both "to surrender" and "to be unfettered." For this reason the person who "surrenders" is called a Muslim—the active participle of Islam—for submitting to the will of God. (Islam)

Jainism Among the most ancient active religions in the world, Jainism is an Indian religion distinct from the Vedic tradition that spawned Hinduism. Jainism follows a theology of pacifism and nonviolence, and espouses a supreme respect for all living things.

Jesus Christ The central figure of Christianity.

Judaism The religion and way of life of the Jewish people, deriving from the Tanakh.

Kagura is an ancient Shinto ritual dance. Tradition holds that it once involved actual possession by the kami invoked during the dance; modern expression pays homage to these shamanic elements but does not attempt to produce spirit possession. (Shinto)

Kam. Lust, one of the five evils or vices that lead humans further from God and distract from the path to truth. (Sikhism)

Karma Action regarded as triggering inevitable good or bad results for the person who performs it, either in this life or in a later incarnation. (Buddhism, Hinduism)

Krodh Rage, one of the five evils or vices that lead humans further from God and distract from the path to truth. (Sikhism)

Lent A 40-day period preceding Easter that emphasizes self-examination and self-denial. (Christianity)

Lobh Greed, one of the five evils or vices that lead humans further from God and distract from the path to truth. (Sikhism)

Mahayana school The dominant form of Buddhism in northern Asia. A branch of Buddhism whose followers believe the Buddha to embody a cosmic "inconceivable" aspect of being, and to have been born for the benefit of other beings. (Buddhism)

Mantra A sound or group of words repeated with the aim of creating or supporting a spiritual transformation.

Misogi A purification ritual using water. It is typically performed by Shinto worshippers before entering a shrine. (Shinto)

Moh Attachment, one of the five evils or vices that lead humans further from God and distract from the path to truth. (Sikhism)

Monotheism The worship of a single God. Major faith systems whose adherents describe themselves as monotheistic include Judaism, Christianity, and Islam.

Muhammad The prophet of Islam. Born in 570 CE, died in 632 CE. (Islam)

Nature-focused faith systems These faiths are often grouped together using variations on the label *pagan*, though how that term is viewed is a complex topic that varies greatly from community to community and individual to individual. Some embrace the *pagan* or *neopagan* label, while others seek to avoid it and the religious and social baggage it carries.

The Nicene Creed. This statement of faith established the formal Trinitarian doctrine of Christianity, which regards God the Father, God the Son, and God the Holy Spirit as Divine. (Christianity)

Nimrata Humility, one of the five virtues that bring humans closer to God. (Sikhism)

Nirvana One popular answer to the question "What is Nirvana?" sounds like this: "A beam of light that never lands anywhere." There are many other answers to consider. (Buddhism)

Northern Taoists (active in China outside of the southern part of the country and Taiwan) They claim a different, somewhat later lineage than Southern Taoists, and de-emphasize public healings and exorcisms. Their practice is more likely to emphasize spiritual and moral development on the personal level.

Orthodox Judaism Of all the Jewish movements, the Orthodox movement is, as the name suggests, the most traditional in its practices. Orthodox Jews accept the entire Torah as the definitive guide for modern life. (Judaism)

Orthodoxy Correctness in belief.

Orthopraxy Correctness in action or practice. Orthopraxy emphasizes ethical conduct in a religious and social context. It stands in contrast to orthodoxy, which emphasizes correct belief. Orthopraxy could also be described as the position that holds correct behavior to be at least as important as the acceptance of the correct religious belief system.

Palm Sunday This holiday celebrates Jesus's entry into Jerusalem. A springtime holiday, it is generally observed in early April. Western and Eastern Christian churches take differing approaches to setting the date. (Christianity)

Pantheism The worship of the Universe (or Nature) in all its manifestations, or the belief that everything is divine.

Pentecost Celebrated 40 days after Easter, this holiday celebrates the coming of the Holy Spirit. (Christianity)

Polytheism The worship of many gods.

Pope The Bishop of Rome and the global leader of the Catholic Church. (Christianity)

Protestant Reformation A rift in Western Christianity that had many precursors, but that took shape in 1517 with the posting of Martin Luther's 95 theses. Luther and others described themselves as reformers who protested the practices, structure, and authority of the Roman Catholic Church. The movement led to the formation of new Protestant churches that rejected the authority of the Pope. (Christianity)

Punjab A region of the northern Indian subcontinent. Sikhism, a global faith, is closely tied to the culture and history the Punjab. (Sikhism)

Pyare Love, one of the five virtues that bring humans closer to God. (Sikhism)

Qur'an The holy text of Islam. (Islam)

Rabbi A teacher who has been adequately educated in Jewish law and tradition. This education allows him to teach and advise the community according to Jewish Law.

The Rastafari movement Based loosely on Judeo-Christian traditions, followers of this faith call God by the name Jah, a contraction of *Jehovah*. Its theology focuses on African culture, and preaches that Africans are God's chosen people, that their rightful place in society has been repressed by European intervention and suppression, and that one day they will be reinstated by Jah.

Reform Judaism Considered the most liberal movement of modern Judaism, Reform Judaism is popular in the United Kingdom and North America. Reform Jews believe the Torah to be the product of different human authors, whose work was then combined. As a result, they hold that traditional Jewish Law is subject to critical evaluation and are more likely to interpret that law as a body of broad guidelines rather than as a set of binding restrictions on Jewish behavior. (Judaism)

Reincarnation The rebirth of the soul in a new body after death. (Buddhism, Hinduism)

Salat The practice of formal Islamic prayer, involving standing, bowing, and prostration in prescribed routines. It is mandatory, five times a day, with a few exceptions (such as for menstruating women, who are excused from it, and for travelers, who may combine certain prayers). (Islam)

Samadhi A level of concentrated meditation that can be described as a state of consciousness in which the consciousness of the observer becomes one with the consciousness of that which is observed. (Buddhism)

Samsara One translation from Sanskrit to English defines this as "continuous movement." The goal of Buddhism in its most basic essence is to find an escape from this powerful cycle of life, death, and rebirth. (Buddhism)

Sanskrit The ancient language of Hinduism and Buddhism.

Santeria A Caribbean religion that mixes the beliefs of the Yoruba people (from parts of Nigeria, Benin, and Togo in Africa) with aspects of Roman Catholicism.

Santokh Contentment, one of the five virtues that bring humans closer to God. (Sikhism)

Sant-Sipahi "Saint-soldier." Sikhs are taught to embody the virtues of the Sant-Sipahi by cultivating a love for and awareness of God, and by showing personal courage in the face of injustice. (Sikhism)

Sat Truth, one of the five virtues that bring humans closer to God. (Sikhism)

Sawm Ramadan Fasting during the month of Ramadan. Abstaining from food, drink, and sexual intercourse is mandatory for all Muslims during the holy month of Ramadan, although exceptions to the fasting are made for the ill, for menstruating and pregnant women, and for travelers. (Islam)

Sewa Similar to the concept of charity in other faith systems. Sewa requires service to others without consideration for oneself. Services are supposed to be rendered to God through connection to all people. (Sikhism)

Shahadah The belief or confession of faith. (Islam)

Shaktism A great devotional school within Hinduism. Its object of veneration is the ancient goddess figure Shakti, also known as Devi or Parvati, the Divine Mother, celebrated as the "one without a second." (Hinduism)

Sharia Commonly but wrongly translated as "Islamic law," Sharia, is ethics. Literally *Sharia* means "a path," and technically it means "that which is revealed." Muslim scholars try to make sense of God's revelation and the Prophet Muhammad's teachings using reason and other modes of interpretation. Ethics deal with the duties owed to God and the reciprocal claims and duties between humans. So Muslim ethics rely on a commitment to God, an obligation to reason, and the need to obtain the greatest good. Sometimes Muslims also use the term *fiqh*, meaning "understanding," interchangeably with Sharia.

Shavism. Also known as Saivism. Reveres the god Shiva as "creator, preserver, destroyer, revealer and concealer of all that is," according to its adherents. (Hinduism)

Shia See *Denominations in Islam.*

Shinto An indigenous spiritual practice of the people of Japan. The word comes from the Chinese words *Shen* ("spirits, natural forces, gods") and *Tao* ("way, path"). It thus means "The path of the spirits" or "The path of the gods." (Shinto)

Sikhism A monotheistic faith system founded during the fifteenth century in the Punjab region of the Indian subcontinent.

Simran This describes a commitment to individual contemplation and meditation on both God and yourself, in the hopes of understanding the Truth of God more completely. (Sikhism)

Southern Taoists A group active in southern China and Taiwan claiming a lineage extending to the Cheng-i tradition, which can be traced back to the eleventh century. Priests in this school perform a liturgy that is held to bring the community into harmony with the Tao. They also perform special healing ceremonies and even public exorcisms.

Sunnah The teachings and example of the Prophet Muhammad. (Islam)

Sunni See *Denominations in Islam*.

Sutras Brief sayings meant to preserve a given piece of instruction relating or convey some other important teaching. (Buddhism, Hinduism)

Synagogue A Jewish house of prayer. (Judaism)

Tanakh Distinctive Hebrew term for Judaism's core religious scriptures, beginning with the book of Genesis (Hebrew: Bere'sit, for "in the beginning [He] created") and ending with the book of Chronicles (Hebrew: Dibh're Hayyamim, for "the matters [of] the days"). It is also known as the Hebrew Bible. The Tanakh comprises the *Torah* (the first five books), the *Nevi'in* (books about various prophets), and the *Ketuvim* (a catchall term literally meaning "writings" applied to a later group of scriptures not included in the first two categories). The word *TaNaKh* is an ancient acronym of the Hebrew names of these three collections. (Judaism)

The Tao This can be defined as the fundamental principle underlying the universe, "the way things are." This one word, endlessly influential in Oriental thought and religious practice, combines within itself the complementary principles of yin (female, negative, dark) and yang (male, positive, bright) energy, and also identifies the Way, or code of behavior, that harmoniously aligns with the natural order of things. (Taoism)

The Tao Te Ching The shortest, most ambiguous of the world's great sacred texts. It emerged in China in a period of deep antiquity. The title can be translated in any number of ways, including "The Great Book of the Way and the Power." (Taoism)

Taoism A religion and a philosophical movement deriving from the ancient texts of the *Tao Te Ching* and the *Zhuangzi*.

Theravada school The oldest surviving identifiable branch of Buddhist practice. It has been the dominant mode of religious expression in Sri Lanka and much of Southeast Asia for many centuries, and has something like 150 million followers worldwide. Theravada Buddhists consider the Buddha a human who, through human striving, attained Nirvana. (Buddhism)

Torah The first five books of the Hebrew Scriptures. (Judaism)

The Trinity An important doctrine of mainstream Christianity identifying "one God in three persons"—God the Father, God the Son, and God the Holy Spirit. Most, but not all, Christians accept the doctrine of the Trinity. (Christianity)

Udasis Important missionary journeys undertaken by Guru Nanak in order to spread his spiritual message. (Sikhism)

Universalism The belief that there are religious, philosophical, and theological principles that have universal applicability, regardless of social or sectarian differences. (The Baha'i Faith)

Upanishads A diverse collection of philosophical observations, initially conveyed in an oral tradition and compiled at various points in history. (Hinduism)

Vaishnavism Also known as Vaisnavism. Reveres the god Vishnu (and his many manifestations) as the original and all-powerful God. This reverence takes place from different points of view and through different traditions, appealing to God by such names as Narayana, Krishna, Vāsudeva, and, of course, Vishnu. (Hinduism)

Vajrayana Buddhism Also known as Tibetan Buddhism and Diamond Vehicle Buddhism, it is thought to have arisen in India in the sixth or seventh century BCE—perhaps a thousand years after the passing of the Buddha. Believers hold, however, that this school's doctrines are in fact directly traceable to a tradition of secret teachings attributable directly to the Buddha. (Buddhism)

Vedas These are the oldest surviving examples of Indian literature and the oldest scriptures of Hinduism. They can be broken down into four separate texts, three of which (the Rigveda, the Yajurveda, and the Samaveda) relate to early Vedic sacrificial rites, and one of which (the Atharaveda) features hymns, spells, incantations, and other material. (Hinduism)

Wu-wei A central concept in Taoism. Literally, it means "nonaction" or "nondoing." The principle has also been rendered as *wei-wu-wei*, meaning "action without actions." A flower that grows, a river that flows, a planet that orbits—all of these phenomena take place in the natural order of things, without conscious effort. (Taoism)

Yoga An umbrella term describing a wide variety of mental, physical, and spiritual disciplines, all deriving from in ancient India and all meant to deliver a state of permanent peace. (Hinduism)

Zakat Alms or charitable giving. This is a preset, mandatory tax upon wealth that is seen as purifying one's wealth. Optional charity (sadaqa) falls under a different category. (Islam)

The *Zhuangzi* The second foundational text of the Taoist philosophical and religious tradition. It is also the name of the author of the text. (Taoism)

Bibliography

Abrahamov, Binyamin, ed., *The Blackwell Companion to the Qur'an*; Blackwell Companions to Religion, Oxford: Blackwell, 2006.

Abu-Hamdiyyah, Mohammad, *The Qur'an: An Introduction*; New York: Routledge, 2000.

Ali, Yusuf, *The Meaning of the Holy Qur'an*; English and Arabic Edition, Beltsville, Maryland: Amana Publications, 1997.

BBC Religions, http://www.bbc.co.uk/religion/religions/judaism/history/abraham_1.shtml.

Beckerlegge, Gwilym, ed., *World Religions Reader*, 2nd ed.; New York: Routledge, 2001.

Berenbaum, Michael, and Fred Skolnik *Encyclodpaedia Judaica*, http://www.bjeindy.org/resources/library/access-to-encyclopedia-judaica/.

Bhikkhu, Thanissaro, Access to Insight, http://www.accesstoinsight.org/lib/authors/thanissaro/samsara.html.

Bible Gateway, http://www.biblegateway.com/passage/?search=Matthew+6%3A9-13&version=KJV.

Bible Hub by Biblos. http://biblehub.com/romans/11-13.htm.

Bowker, John, *The Oxford Dictionary of World Religions*; New York: Oxford University Press, 1997.

Brockopp, Jonathan E., ed., *Cambridge Companion to Muhammad*, series: Cambridge Companions to Religion; Cambridge: Cambridge University Press, 2010.

Brown, Jonathan A. C., *Mohammad: A Very Short Introduction*; New York: Oxford University Press, 2011.

Buddha Groove, http://www.buddhagroove.com/readings/listings/what-does-samadhi-mean/.

Burke, T. Patrick, *The Major Religions*; Cambridge, MA: Blackwell Publishers, 1996.

Carrithers, Michael, *The Buddha: A Very Short Introduction*; New York: Oxford University Press, 2001.

Chidester, David, *Christianity: A Global History*; San Francisco: HarperSan Francisco, 2000.

Cole, W. Owen, and Piara Singh Sambhi, *A Popular Dictionary of Sikhism*; New York: Routledge, 1997.

Congregation B'nai Shalom, http://bshalom.org/lifelong-learning/torah-school/.

Conze, Edward, *Buddhism: A Short History*; Oxford: One World, 2000.

Coogan, Michael, ed., *The Illustrated Guide to World Religions*; New York: Oxford University Press, 2003.

Cook, Michael, *The Koran: A Very Short Introduction*; New York: Oxford University Press, 2000.

Cousins, Ewert, ed., *World Spirituality: An Encyclopedic History of the Religious Quest*; New York: Crossroad, 1985.

Cush, Denise, Catherine Robinson, and Michael York, eds., *Encyclopedia of Hinduism*; New York: Routledge, 2007.

Davies, W. D., and Louis Finkelstein, *The Cambridge History of Judaism*; New York: Cambridge University Press, 1989.

de Lange, Nicholas, *An Introduction to Judaism*; Cambridge University Press, 2000.

Dhahabi, Imam Shamsu ed-Deen, *Major Sins*, http://www.islamguiden.com/arkiv/majorsins.pdf.

Diffen contributers, DiffenLLC, http://www.diffen.com/difference/Buddhism_vs_Hinduism.

Donner, Fred M., *Muhammad and the Believers: At the Origins of Islam*; Cambridge, MA: Harvard University Press, 2010.

Eger, Denise L., Congregation Kol Nidre, https://www.kol-ami.org/article.aspx?id=10737419923&blogid=10737418339.

English Tourism, The Three Jewels of the Tao, http://202.119.208.181/G2S/Template/View.aspx?wmz=18844&courseType=1&courseId=30&topMenuId=1064&menuType=4&contentId=18844&action=view&type=&name=&linkpageID=69287.

Esposito, John L. ed., *The Oxford Dictionary of Islam*; New York: Oxford University Press, 2002.

Esposito, John L., *The Oxford History of Islam*; New York: Oxford University Press, 2000.

Esposito, John, Darrell Fasching, and Todd Lewis, eds., *World Religions Today*; New York: Oxford University Press, 2001.

Evinity Publishing INC, Sacred Texts, http://www.sacred-texts.com/tao/tt/tt03.htm.

Finest Quotes, http://www.finestquotes.com/author_quotes-author-Sri%20 Aurobindo-page-0.htm.

Flood, Gavin, *An Introduction to Hinduism*; New York: Cambridge University Press, 1996.

Gilley, Sheridan and Brian Stanley, *The Cambridge History of Christianity*; vol. 8, Cambridge, New York: Cambridge University Press, 2005.

Goodman, Martin, Jeremy Cohen, and David Sorkin, eds., *The Oxford Handbook of Jewish Studies*; New York: Oxford University Press, 2003.

GoodReads, https://www.goodreads.com/quotes/547111-there-is-a-way-that-nature-speaks-that-land-speaks.

Harvey, Peter, *An Introduction to Buddhism*; New York: Cambridge University Press, 1990.

Hastings, Adrian, ed., *A World History of Christianity*; Grand Rapids, Michigan, Eerdmans, 2000.

Hinnells, John Red, *A New Dictionary of Religions*; Cambridge, MA: Blackwell Publishers, 1997.

Hinnells, John Red, *A New Handbook of Living Religions*; Cambridge, MA: Blackwell Publishers, 1997.

Honcho, Jinja, Jinja Honcho Association of Shinto Shrines, http://www.jinjahoncho.or.jp/en/festival/.

Hopfe, Lewis M., *Religions of the World*, 6th ed.; New York: Macmillan College Publishing, 1994.

ISKCON Educational Services, The Heart of Hinduism, http://hinduism.iskcon.org/tradition/1201.htm.

ISKCON Educational Services, The Heart of Hinduism, http://hinduism.iskcon.org/tradition/1203.htm.

Jacobs, Louis, ed., *The Jewish Religion: A Companion*; New York: Oxford University Press, 1995.

Juergensmeyer, Mark, *Global Religions: An Introduction*; New York: Oxford University Press, 2003.

Keown, Damien, *Buddhism: A Very Short Introduction*; New York: Oxford University Press, 2000.

Knott, Kim, *Hinduism: A Very Short Introduction*; New York: Oxford University Press, 2000.

Lewis, C. S., GoodReads, https://www.goodreads.com/quotes/6979-i-am-trying-here-to-prevent-anyone-saying-the-really.

Loon Watch, http://www.loonwatch.com/2010/01/not-all-terrorists-are-muslims/.

Lowe, Bryan, Cross Quotes, http://crossquotes.org/category/andrew-murray-quotes/.

Markham, Ian S, ed., *A World Religions Reader*; Cambridge, MA: Blackwell Publishers, 1996.

Matthews, Warren, *World Religions*; St. Paul, MN: West Publishing Company 1991.

Maven, Ana, The Attractive Arts, http://theattractivearts.com/resources/movie-reviews/the-tao-of-steve/.

McAuliffe, Jane Dammen, ed., *The Cambridge Companion to the Qur'an*, Cambridge Companions to Religion; New York: Cambridge University Press, 2006.

McManners, John, ed., *The Oxford Illustrated History of Christianity*; Oxford: Oxford University Press, 1990.

Neusner, Jacob, and Alan J. Avery-Peck, eds., *The Blackwell Companion to Judaism*; Oxford: Blackwell, 2000.

Nuesner, Jacob, ed., *World Religions in America: An Introduction*, rev. and expanded ed.; Louisville, KY: Westminster John Knox, 1999.

O'Conner, Kevin, Find the Data, http://famous-quotes.findthedata.org/l/96190/Hinduism-s-basic-tenet-is-that-many-roads-ex-Kenneth-Scott-Latourette.

OSHO International Foundation, OSHO Online Library, http://www.osho.com/library/online-library-seed-nirvana-substratum-cb95d5cf-c20.aspx.

Oxtoby, Willard G., ed., *World Religions*, vol. 1: *Western Traditions*, vol. 2: *Eastern Traditions*, 2nd ed.; New York: Oxford University Press, 2001.

Patheos Library, http://www.patheos.com/Library/Zen.html.

Pearl S. Buck, Quotes http://www.psbi.org/document.doc?id=271.

Quote Japan, http://quotejapan.wordpress.com/ronald-p-dore-quotes-from-%E2%80%9Cshinohata-a-portrait-of-a-japanese-village%E2%80%9D-1978/.

Qur'an Explorer, http://quranexplorer.com/index/Sura_096_Al_Alaq_THE_CLOT_READ.aspx.

Reninger, Elizabeth, About.com, http://taoism.about.com/od/qi/a/Qi.htm.

Reninger, Elizabeth, About.com, http://taoism.about.com/od/chuangtzu/a/ Butterfly_Dream.htm.

Ruthven, Malise, *Islam: A Very Short Introduction*; New York: Oxford University Press, 2000.

Ryden, Edmund, and Benjamine Penny, trans., *Laozi: Daodejing*, Oxford World Classics; New York: Oxford University Press, 2008.

Sardar, Ziauddin, *Reading the Qur'an: The Contemporary Relevance of the Sacred Text of Islam*; New York: Oxford University, 2011.

Solomon, Norman, *Judaism: A Very Short Introduction*; New York: Oxford University Press, 2000.

V., Jayaram Saivism.net, http://www.saivism.net/.

Waines, David, *An Introduction to Islam*; New York: Cambridge University Press, 1995.

Wang, Keping, *Reading the Dao: A Thematic Inquiry*; New York: Continuum International, 2011.

Warrior Poet Wisdom, http://warriorpoetwisdom.com/tag/samurai/.

Werblowsky, R. J. Zwi, and Geoffrey Wigoder, eds., *Oxford Dictionary of Judaism*; New York: Oxford University Press, 1997.

Wikipedia, http://en.wikipedia.org/wiki/Karma_in_Hinduism.

Wilberg, Peter, The New Yoga, http://www.thenewyoga.org/Hinduism.pdf.

Young, William A, *The World's Religions: Worldviews and Contemporary Issues*; Engelwood Cliffs, NJ: Prentice-Hall Inc., 1995.

Zweig, Connie, GoodReads, https://www.goodreads.com/author/quotes/106272. Connie_Zweig.

Answer Key

CHAPTER 1

1. B   2. B   3. D   4. B   5. C   6. A   7. A   8. B   9. D   10. D

CHAPTER 2

1. A   2. C   3. A   4. A   5. C   6. A   7. B   8. A   9. A   10. B

CHAPTER 3

1. C   2. A   3. C   4. C   5. B   6. B   7. A   8. B   9. True   10. A

CHAPTER 4

1. B   2. A   3. B   4. C   5. D   6. C   7. D   8. False   9. False   10. B

CHAPTER 5

1. C   2. A   3. A   4. B   5. B   6. B   7. A   8. B   9. True   10. False

CHAPTER 6

1. A   2. C   3. A   4. C   5. False   6. A   7. A   8. C   9. C   10. B

CHAPTER 7

1. B   2. D   3. A   4. B   5. D   6. A   7. A   8. True   9. A   10. B

CHAPTER 8

1. A   2. B   3. B   4. C   5. B   6. B   7. C   8. A   9. True   10. True

PART ONE TEST

1. A   2. D   3. A   4. True   5. A   6. A   7. C   8. A   9. D   10. D
11. A   12. C   13. B   14. B   15. A   16. B   17. C   18. C   19. C   20. D
21. C   22. A   23. B   24. A   25. B   26. A   27. A   28. C   29. C   30. A
31. A   32. A   33. A   34. True   35. A   36. C

CHAPTER 9

1. A   2. B   3. C   4. A   5. A   6. B   7. B   8. B   9. False   10. A

CHAPTER 10

1. B   2. A   3. C   4. A   5. B   6. A   7. A   8. B   9. C   10. True

CHAPTER 11

1. A   2. B   3. A   4. C   5. A   6. B   7. A   8. C   9. A   10. B

CHAPTER 12

1. C   2. A   3. C   4. A   5. B   6. A   7. D   8. B   9. False   10. False

CHAPTER 13

1. B   2. B   3. A   4. C   5. A   6. B   7. C   8. A   9. B   10. C

CHAPTER 14

1. C   2. C   3. D   4. D   5. A   6. C   7. A   8. D   9. A   10. False

PART TWO TEST

1. C   2. A   3. B   4. False   5. A   6. B   7. A   8. B   9. C   10. B   11. D
12. A   13. B   14. B   15. C   16. A   17. C   18. A   19. A   20. A   21. A
22. B   23. A   24. C   25. B   26. D   27. A   28. B   29. True   30. A

CHAPTER 15

1. C   2. B   3. C   4. A   5. A   6. C   7. D   8. C   9. False   10. True

CHAPTER 16

1. A   2. A   3. B   4. B   5. A   6. B   7. A   8. A   9. C   10. True

CHAPTER 17

1. C   2. C   3. B   4. A   5. C   6. A   7. B   8. A   9. A   10. B

PART THREE TEST

1. A   2. D   3. B   4. B   5. A   6. B   7. A   8. C   9. A   10. B   11. A
12. B   13. C   14. A   15. C   16. A   17. C   18. B   19. A   20. C   21. D
22. B   23. D   24. B   25. A

FINAL EXAM

1. A   2. C   3. B   4. False   5. C   6. A   7. C   8. C   9. A   10. A   11. B
12. C   13. A   14. B   15. A   16. C   17. A   18. C   19. C   20. A   21. C
22. A   23. B   24. C   25. B   26. True   27. A   28. C   29. C   30. C   31. True
32. A   33. C   34. B   35. C   36. B   37. A   38. C   39. B   40. D   41. A   42. A
43. A   44. B   45. C   46. C   47. C   48. B   49. C   50. True   51. B   52. True
53. B   54. B   55. A   56. A   57. C   58. A   59. C   60. B   61. C   62. True
63. C   64. A   65. B   66. C   67. C   68. A   69. B   70. C   71. D   72. A   73. B
74. A   75. C   76. A   77. B   78. A   79. A   80. B   81. C   82. C   83. C   84. B
85. A   86. B   87. A   88. A   89. False   90. D   91. C   92. B   93. A   94. B
95. B   96. A   97. A   98. False   99. C   100. A

Index